M000280495

"The New Testament of hope and love. It is called colleague Kris Vallotton community to help shape, Prophets.' Thanks for honoring my generation's pioneering work and picking up the baton and carrying it forth!"

Dr. James Goll, founder, Encounters Network, Prayer Storm and GET eSchool; author, *The Seer*, *The Lifestyle of a Prophet*, *Praying for Israel's Destiny* and many more

"My precious friend Kris Vallotton has masterfully crafted this treatise, *School of the Prophets*, on the dynamics and framework of building a prophetic community in the 21st century. His life experience and seasoning in Christ have afforded the Spirit the opportunity to make him an influencer of influencers and a prohetic voice to the nations with a global footprint."

Mark J. Chironna, M.A., Ph.D.; Mark Chironna Ministries; Church on the Living Edge, Orlando, Florida

"*School of the Prophets* is a much-needed resource for those desiring to grow in prophecy and those desiring to understand it. I love this book and will highly recommend it to my students in the prophetic."

Patricia King, founder, XP Ministries

"I *love* this book! As a person passionate to see the most desired gift in the New Testament (see 1 Corinthians 14:1) flourish all over the world, I would recommend this book wholesale. It clearly and biblically describes how to function in the New Testament gift of prophecy and articulates various kinds of biblical prophets. If one heeds its principles, it will give greater understanding and produce higher levels of maturity in prophetic ministry. 'I wish that all the LORD's people were prophets' (Numbers 11:29 NIV) and that they all read Kris Vallotton's great book *School of the Prophets*."

Stacey Campbell, founder, Canadian Prophetic Council; author, *Ecstatic Prophecy*

"This is a must-read for all ministries. As an apostolic ministry, we recognize the gifts and callings that God has placed on the lives of those we pastor. Reading *School of the Prophets* has given us greater insight and understanding of how to help develop and prepare others to walk in their divine assignment. Kris Vallotton brings much clarity in what it means to be called in the office of a prophet and eliminates the fear of giving and receiving the prophetic."

Tony and Cynthia Brazelton, founders and pastors,
Victory Christian Ministries International

"Kris Vallotton's book reminds us that the heart of prophecy should be God's heart to build up, encourage and speak life. God sees the greatness over our lives, and our desire should be to see each other as He does. Kris goes through strategic and important teaching about prophecy versus the office of prophet, specifically in the context of the Church. I highly recommend this book and pray that it helps you to understand the prophetic and to 'call the gold' out of those around you. Our whole family has been uplifted in a powerful way through our deep friendship with this amazing man."

Heidi Baker, Ph.D.; co-founder and director, Iris Global

"As I read this book, I could hear the sound of an entire genereation of voices emerge that will transform culture. Kris Vallotton is a father to these voices. As a relational prophet, Kris teaches us what he knows but also reproduces who he is. *School of the Prophets* presents a practical methodology for prophetic community and a powerful manifesto for prophetic transformation in this generation."

Bob Hazlett, author, *The Roar: God's Sound in a Raging World*; www.bobhazlett.org;
Future Perspectives, New Haven, Connecticut

SCHOOL OF THE PROPHETS

Other Books and Materials by Kris Vallotton

Developing a Supernatural Lifestyle: A Practical Guide to a Life of Signs, Wonders, and Miracles

Fashioned to Reign: Empowering Women to Fulfill Their Divine Destiny (book, workbook, leader's guide and video segments available, or an all-inclusive curriculum kit)

God's Most Beautiful Creation (a six-part DVD or CD teaching series on women)

Heavy Rain: Renew the Church, Transform the World

Moral Revolution: The Naked Truth about Sexual Purity

Outrageous Courage: What God Can Do with Raw Obedience and Radical Faith (the Tracy Evans story; co-authored with Jason Vallotton)

School of the Prophets Curriculum Kit (includes a workbook, leader's guide and video segments; these components can also be purchased individually)

Spirit Wars: Winning the Invisible Battle against Sin and the Enemy (book, workbook, leader's guide and video segments available, or an all-inclusive curriculum kit)

The Supernatural Power of Forgiveness: Discover How to Escape Your Prison of Pain and Unlock a Life of Freedom (co-authored with Jason Vallotton)

The Supernatural Ways of Royalty: Discovering Your Rights and Privileges of Being a Son or Daughter of God (co-authored with Bill Johnson)

Basic Training for the Supernatural Ways of Royalty (workbook)

Basic Training for the Prophetic Ministry (workbook)

School

OF THE

PROPHETS

Advanced Training for Prophetic Ministry

KRIS VALLOTTON

Chosen

a division of Baker Publishing Group
Minneapolis, Minnesota

Published by Chosen Books
11400 Hampshire Avenue South
Bloomington, Minnesota 55438
www.chosenbooks.com

Chosen Books is a division of
Baker Publishing Group, Grand Rapids, Michigan

Printed in the United States of America

Library of Congress Cataloging-in-Publication Data
Vallotton, Kris
    School of the prophets : advanced training for prophetic ministry / Kris Vallotton.
      pages cm
    Includes index.
    Summary: "This essential guide to the prophetic reveals the often-ignored foundational truths pivotal to prophetic ministry, provides critical advanced training, and helps readers grow in their giftings"— Provided by publisher.
     ISBN 978-0-8007-9620-4 (pbk. : alk. paper)
     1. Gifts, Spiritual. 2. Prophecy—Christianity. I. Title.
BT767.3.V35 2015
234′.13—dc23   2014032033

Cover design by Dan Pitts

15 16 17 18 19 20 21   7 6 5 4 3 2 1

I dedicate this book to the prophets and prophetesses who went before us and paved the way for our success with their extreme sacrifice under much religious persecution. I especially want to thank Larry Randolph, who has been a great role model to me, particularly in the early years of my prophetic development. I also want to thank Bob Jones. Bob was a father to me and helped me through the worst season of my entire life. I am eternally indebted to him. Bob Jones has recently gone on to be with the Lord, and I miss him so much.

I also want to dedicate this book to Bill Johnson, who taught me how to value the prophetic ministry. Bill has been my leader for nearly four decades and has always been patient with me as I struggled through countless mistakes to grow in my prophetic call.

And finally, I want to dedicate this book to Kathy, who is the woman of my dreams. She encouraged me when I wanted to quit, stood by me when life was painful and has been my best friend and lover since she was twelve years old. She is the most loyal and noble person I have ever known, and without her I would have nothing to say.

CONTENTS

FOREWORD

About thirty years ago, I was privileged to spend some time with one of the greatest heroes of my life. He was probably forty years my senior and had experienced things in God I had only dreamed of. I still pass along some of the stories I heard that day. Our conversation ranged from revival, to the move of the Spirit in a meeting, to miracles, and many similar topics. His answers were the most insightful I had ever heard. My life has been forever changed.

When I asked him about prophets and the prophetic—as that had captured my attention in recent years—he gave me priceless insights and counsel through his experiences in that area. But his bottom-line counsel for me was to leave it alone, as it would only bring division to the church.

His counsel was pastoral in nature and important for me to hear. He had witnessed a movement in which marriages were prophesied into existence, only to fail. Others were sent overseas by a prophetic word as missionaries when God had never called them. Disappointment and bewilderment were the results. Such horror stories seemed to be endless, as he obviously still bore the sting of the prophetic gone wrong.

While it may seem like a contradiction, his counsel encouraged me to pursue the very thing he warned me against, but to do so with unusual emphasis on wisdom.

I already had good relationships with several legitimate prophets who were lovers of the church and submitted their gift to the scrutiny of others. The fruit of their ministries was unmistakable. I have personally received ministry countless times from these gifted people, always with supernatural fruit. Besides, my friend's warning only emphasized to me that the devil is a counterfeiter.

Have you noticed that counterfeiters never counterfeit pennies? It is not worth the effort. They counterfeit larger bills because of their value. In the same way, whatever the devil tries to destroy, counterfeit or dilute only reveals what he fears the most. That means the prophetic done right frightens the powers of darkness—and is, therefore, tremendously necessary.

And so the journey began. We experimented in small groups, where it was easy to clean up our messes, when we made them. We also kept it among the people we knew the best so they would keep us accountable. We basically made an agreement that because this was dangerous, staying humble and accountable was the only way we could pursue something of such danger—and value.

During that season Kris Vallotton began to emerge. His gift was clear and strong yet unrefined. No one, in any gift, starts refined. To reject someone because he does not use a gift with maturity only reveals the immaturity of the mentor. We had to make room for all of us to learn. And learn we did.

Fast forward 30-plus years: It is one of my greatest honors to present to you my friend and ministry partner for the past

35 years, a true prophet of God, Kris Vallotton. Kris has learned how to communicate what the Lord is saying, not from a place of shame or condemnation but from a place of hope, life and encouragement. The focus of his ministry is on what God is doing—which often contrasts with the bent of many prophets who see mainly what is wrong with the world or the Church.

This book is the result of decades of personal training and learning. I consider it to be a priceless treasure of lessons learned, some the hard way, but learned for sure.

I have had the privilege to know and share life with many true prophets of God through the years. They are gifts to the church and treasures to me personally. Yet I have never met anyone who carries such a strong grace to train others in the ministry of being a prophet or in operating in the gift of prophecy as Kris does. His training is clear, risky, powerful and extremely fruitful.

This book reveals the very life and heart of the Father, looking to equip and lead others into their place of contribution to His purposes on the earth, giving hope to the Church "for such a time as this."

I watched this book being written on the tablet of Kris's heart long before it ever reached this printing. And so you hold in your hands a book that will forever leave a mark on the way you approach your gift, whether you are a prophet or even if you have never prophesied. This book is useful for every person with any spiritual gift.

Bill Johnson, senior leader, Bethel Church,
Redding, California; author, *When Heaven Invades Earth*,
Experience the Impossible and more; co-author,
The Essential Guide to Healing and *Healing Unplugged*

INTRODUCTION

Navigating White Water

When I was fifteen years old, my mother was sick with psoriasis that covered most of her body. To make matters worse, for nearly a year we had a prowler trying to break into our home, prompting both of us to sleep with a gun by our side at night. The police were staking out our house nearly every night to try to catch the perpetrator. The guy actually got into my bedroom one night. . . . I woke up just in time to see him coming through my window. Half asleep, I pulled out my gun and took a shot at him as he leaped out the window. These were trying times for my family, and as the oldest of three children, I felt as if the weight of the world were on my shoulders.

In the midst of all this chaos, in the wee hours of the morning, lying in my bed, I said out loud, "If there is a God and if You will heal my mother, I will find out who You are and serve You the rest of my life!"

A moment later, an audible voice said, "My name is Jesus Christ, and you have what you requested!"

I always had a sense that there was a God, but I did not know who He was. Nor had I ever had any kind of supernatural experience prior to this. Yet the next morning my mother was completely well, healed of the psoriasis, and within a few more days, the police apprehended the prowler. Needless to say, our life became substantially more peaceful.

About a week passed, and the voice returned again in the middle of the night, saying, "My name is Jesus Christ. You said that if I healed your mother, you would serve Me, and I am waiting!"

For three long years, I searched for Him by going from church to church, looking for the God who had spoken to me. I am not saying that God was not present in those churches, but for whatever reason, I simply did not connect with Him there. Finally, when I was eighteen, my desperate journey came to an end in a house filled with hippies. That night, I gave my heart to Jesus and began to keep my promise to follow Him the rest of my life. It would be years before I would realize that I was part of the Jesus People movement. I was not a hippie or a drug addict. In fact, the truth is that I had never drunk alcohol in my life, and the only person I have ever had sex with is my wife. Yet I connected with the Jesus People so well because I shared their passion for God and their intense curiosity regarding signs and wonders. After all, my entrance into the Kingdom came through an audible invitation.

The Challenging Years

It was not long before my spiritual journey introduced me to two other streams: the charismatic Catholics and the Protestant Pentecostals. The Jesus People, charismatics and

Pentecostals all believed in a supernatural God who still speaks to His people today. But the homogenization of these three cultures was at times confusing, and at times even divisive. Most of the Jesus People had very little theology behind anything they did. Like me, they came into the Kingdom through some kind of supernatural encounter, which often happened outside the Church. Their paradigm for God was therefore nearly 100 percent experience oriented. Their prophecies were free-flowing, boundaryless and often unbiblical. But they had good hearts, and they wanted desperately to please God. The Jesus People also had been taught a very negative eschatology. This created a rapture mentality and a pretty intense fear of the devil, the Beast and his mark. This often filtered into their prophecies, which were filled with words about Jesus returning at any moment.

The charismatic Catholics often had some theological foundation, but it was usually based more on tradition than on the Bible itself. The Catholics' end time perspective has always been positive, so their prophetic words were not usually filled with rapture fantasies and/or mark of the Beast references. But they were obsessed with the Holy Spirit and spoke of Him in the first person, as if He were a friend sitting next to them. They believed that He had given them gifts to use whenever they wanted. Their prophetic style was not quite as free-flowing as the Jesus People, but their prophetic delivery was also very casual and not usually very dramatic.

On the other hand, the Pentecostals were a completely different bunch. They prophesied only when the "Holy Ghost" anointed them to speak. If they did not speak at the moment He "anointed" them, they felt that they had quenched the Spirit. They had deep theological convictions about the moving of the Holy Ghost that were often based on a mixture of the Old Testament prophets, with some New Testament

Scriptures added in for flavor. They almost always spoke in tongues before they prophesied, and their prophecies usually began with, "Thus saith the Lord." Of course, they only read the King James Version of the Bible, so almost every prophecy sounded like a line from a Shakespearean play, with nearly as much drama.

These three streams often flowed into one pool at conferences and special gatherings. As you can imagine, the meetings were not always harmonious. Then, a few years after I began following Jesus, Kathy and I met Bill Johnson and he became our leader, as he still is to this day. Bill and his wife, Beni, serve as the senior leaders of Bethel Church in Redding, California. Bill has always had an interesting perspective on the prophetic ministry. First of all, he is a fifth-generation Pentecostal leader whose father was a district supervisor in the Assemblies of God. Bill's father, Earl, also pastored Bethel Church during the Jesus People movement, and he loved the charismatic Catholics. He even had charismatic Catholic priests speak to his congregation.

Bill's church and family background not only gave him a diverse perspective on God's supernatural Kingdom, but it also enabled him to gain a deep understanding of these three prophetic streams and to value them. His tendency was to embrace them all and to "eat the meat and spit out the bones," as he would often say to me in our early years together. But what was even more evident in Bill's life was his deep love for the prophets and for the gift of prophecy. Bill literally transcribed every prophetic word he had ever received and took them with him wherever he went. He frequently poured over them, and although there were many prophecies spoken over him and our flock, he knew a lot of them by heart. He rarely made an important decision in his personal life without some sort of prophetic direction. Consequently, this has become one of the core foundational principles of the way we lead our church and our movement to this day.

Herding Cats

Bill's love for diversity has inspired a lot of different kinds of people to follow us. Navigating the white waters of these different prophetic streams as they flow together into one mighty river of revelation can be difficult at best, and at times it is nearly impossible.

I started proactively pastoring our prophetic people about 25 years ago to help bring some sense of sanity and purpose to them. Like Bill, through the years I have learned to enjoy every prophetic stream and the variety of ways that God speaks to people in various epoch seasons, and through diverse cultural experiences and core values. I have come to understand that each of us views the Kingdom through a glass dimly, yet our collective perspectives are much more accurate because revelation is actually a community garden. It is cultivated, seeded, weeded and harvested by a prophetic community and not by an isolated island dweller. It is therefore imperative that prophets and prophetesses develop wholesome prophetic communities that inspire healthy young prophets and prophetic people to be discovered, developed and ultimately deployed into their divine destinies.

The challenge with leading a diverse group of prophetic people is that it is often like herding cats! Although prophets and prophetesses (contrary to popular opinion) do not fit into a personality profile, all of them tend to be extraordinarily sensitive and can easily feel misunderstood and/or rejected. Most of them are not used to having anyone speak into their lives or their ministries, therefore the slightest feedback is often deemed "persecution." To make matters worse, pastors tend to be afraid of people who are extraordinarily prophetically gifted. Pastors commonly feel as though they are not qualified to give such anointed people input into how their ministry is affecting the flock. But prophets and prophetesses desperately need leadership in their lives, and they need input from the other fivefold ministers if they are to stay healthy and nourish prophetic communities.

My Vision

My vision and goal in writing this book is to share with prophets and prophetesses some of the insights that I have learned over the years for how to develop a healthy prophetic community. I want to make it clear that this book is not the final word on prophets and prophetesses, nor is it the only perspective that anyone leading a prophetic community should embrace. I am simply one voice of experience crying out in the wilderness of revelation, trying to help make the crooked prophetic places straight so that Jesus can have a greater impact on our nations.

May God give us wisdom as we navigate the white water of this most exciting and powerful office of the prophet!

DISCOVERING YOUR DIVINE CALL

It all began on a winter day in the Trinity Alps in 1985. The snow covered the forest like a beautiful white sheet, while the sun glistened off every snowflake. I left our Union 76 Station about 6:30 p.m. and forged my way up our relatively steep driveway in our old, green International Scout. The Scout creaked and rattled its way up our dirt road, pushing snow as it rumbled to a stop at the front door of our humble chalet. Our three young children were waiting for me on the front deck, snowballs in hand, while I tromped my way through the deep snow in my rubber boots, defending myself from their onslaughts. The kids giggled and laughed as I quickly overtook them, dropping snowballs on each of their heads.

Then I grabbed the doorknob and retreated into the house, shouting, "Okay, that's enough. . . . No more snowballs. . . .

Come on, now, you'll get your mom upset if you throw one of those into the house!"

I heard snowballs hit the door as I slammed it behind me. The smell of food cooking in the kitchen filled my senses, while the heat from the woodstove warmed my frozen body.

"Hi, baby. How was your day?" I inquired as I made my way into the kitchen.

"Good, honey," she said, leaning over to give me a kiss, her hands full of plates.

"I'm going to jump into the bathtub while you finish dinner," I told her.

"I already filled the tub for you," she said with a smile.

"Thank you, baby," I remarked.

Frankly, I would have been surprised if she had not filled the bathtub, as this was our tradition. She cooked dinner while I soaked in the bathtub for an hour every night after work. I would read my Bible and unwind from a grueling day at the shop by relaxing in our old, claw-foot bathtub. The bathroom was the only room in the house that locked, so it became sort of a place of refuge when one of us needed a break from the kids. When dinner was ready, I would get out of the tub and we would eat together as a family. Then I would play with the kids, and Kathy would get a break from her long day with them.

I grabbed my Bible, its pages tattered from years of steam from the tub, and carefully submerged myself in the hot water. It felt like a thousand needles were poking my frozen feet and legs as my body temperature slowly crept back to normal. As the pain subsided, I read a couple familiar chapters from the Bible, then I closed my eyes, praying silently for the things that concerned my heart. There was nothing particularly special about this night; it was just like any other time in the tub. I read, I prayed, I contemplated, I meditated. . . . It was never a particularly exciting or extraordinarily spiritual time. Personally, I was not prone to mystical experiences or angelic visitations; it was always just a peaceful experience of sensing God's goodness and enjoying a few quiet minutes to myself.

But suddenly, something astonishing happened. I heard a strange noise, and I opened my eyes just in time to see Jesus walk through the wall and stand in front of me! I sat up in the tub with a sense of awe surging through my being like electricity. I looked up into His face, and I could see the world in His eyes. Then, to my surprise, He began to speak to me.

"I have called you to be a prophet to the nations. You will speak before kings and queens. You will influence prime ministers and presidents. I will open doors for you to talk to mayors, governors, ambassadors and government officials all around the world. You will be a father to many nations, and you will guide many nations into prosperity, freedom and peace. I will put My words in your mouth, and the nations will know that there is a God in heaven who loves them, leads them and guides the affairs of men!"

The vision lasted for about half an hour as Jesus told me many other things that would happen in my life. I sat there in the tub, speechless, my mind swirling with thoughts, while my heart trembled with some sort of awesome fear, excitement and wonder all mixed up into one tumultuous emotion.

Finally, the Lord turned His back toward me to leave the room. Then He suddenly stopped, turned back around and pointed right at me. He said in a serious tone, *"History will tell us if you believe Me!"*

A moment later, He was gone.

I lay there for what seemed like an eternity, trying to process what had just happened to me. My mind was at war with itself, proposing a hundred unanswerable questions: *I'm a mechanic and a businessman; how can I be a prophet? I have*

*no education, and I don't know a thing about governments;
why would the leader of a country invite me to speak? If I
were invited, what would I say?*

Then all the "Who am I?" questions began to flood my
mind: *Why would God send a service station owner from
Weaverville to speak to kings and queens? It has only been
two years since I had a serious nervous breakdown—not to
mention the fact that I am terrified of flying—so how the
heck would I even get to another country?*

I could not control my thoughts. Walls of questions and
bars of insecurity imprisoned my soul. Finally, the silence
was broken by Kathy calling out, "Honey, dinner is ready."

I struggled to find the strength to pull myself out of the
bathtub. As I dried off, I decided not to share my extraordinary encounter with anyone for a while. I was concerned
that people would laugh at me behind my back or somehow
think that I considered myself some kind of a big shot or
something. Certainly none of my friends had ever thought of
me as a prophet even to our church, much less to the nations.

I held off telling Kathy for a different reason. She is a
very realistic, "get it done" kind of person. I feared that she
would overwhelm me with practical questions. She would
ask, "How would we make a living ministering to world leaders? What would we do with our business? How could we
travel with small children? Could we do all this while living
in Weaverville?"

I knew she would never want to move out of the mountains.
I also did not have answers for any of my questions, much
less the ones I knew she would start asking, so I decided to
remain silent and try to work it out myself.

Looking back now, I can see that I was so entrenched in
the vision that it was hard for me to be present anywhere. My
emotions were all over the map; one minute I was excited that

God would call somebody like me to guide the nations, and the next minute I was terrified by the thought of standing in front of some ruler and having nothing to say.

In the Meantime

Days turned into months as I remained silent about my encounter with Jesus. I was eager for God to confirm His call on my life through someone else (hopefully someone our church leadership team respected), but no confirmation would come for more than two years. Time passed, and my excitement turned into concern as I began to question whether my visitation was real or just my wild imagination playing some cruel trick on me.

I spent hours reasoning with myself. I knew that I had never fantasized about being a prophet, nor did I ever have any secret dream of influencing kings. The truth is, I had been raised with a poverty mindset, so I pretty much believed that wealthy and/or powerful people were all crooks who could not be trusted. Hence, I reassured myself that I would never dream of being some big-shot prophet, traversing the planet to influence world leaders. After all, my greatest ambition was to own the best automotive repair shop in the world. Yet I could not shake the Lord's intense exhortation: *"History will tell us if you believe Me!"*

I decided to do what I could to steward the word I was given as best I knew how, yet I really was not sure where to start. After all, I did not know anyone who even knew a world leader, much less anyone who had prophesied over them. I decided that I would begin with reading every book I could find that had been written about prophets and prophecy. I poured over each page as if my life depended on it, highlighting every major point and filling several notebooks with the insights I was gaining. At the same time, I read and reread every passage of Scripture having anything to do with prophets and prophecy. My heart was like a sponge, absorbing every bit of revelation I could squeeze out of the Scriptures.

Slowly but surely, something was changing in my spirit. It was as if the vision had somehow sown seeds in the garden of my heart that were growing into some kind of fruitful orchard. I could feel the heavenly vision wrapping its roots around my heart. I envisioned myself like Daniel, serving in the courts of Nebuchadnezzar, guiding the destiny of nations with heavenly visions and prophetic proclamations. There I was, a simple, uneducated man, standing before world leaders, sharing fresh revelation with them straight from the throne room of God. Excitement filled my soul as I imagined presidents stunned by my prophetic words, weeping as they tried to grasp the wisdom from another age. Little did I know that the process to the palace would be much more humbling than I could ever imagine. *Yikes!* But at least I was gaining a passion for something I had never cared about. That in itself was a miracle.

A Prophet in the House

Two long years had passed since I had lain in the bathtub and had the vision of Jesus talking to me about being a prophet to the nations. Then suddenly, I became a magnet that seemed to attract prophetic words everywhere I went. It was as if God had flipped a switch on in heaven that shone a spotlight on me. People began, both publicly and privately, to prophesy amazing words over me about touching nations and ministering to political leaders. During those days, prophets and prophetic people prophesied Proverbs 18:16 over me a number of times: "A man's gift makes room for him and brings him before great men." Thankfully, my church leaders were often present when those words were spoken over me. In fact, several times the declarations came from them.

Jesus said, "A prophet is not without honor except in his hometown and in his own household" (Matthew 13:57), yet something special was happening in the life of our fellowship. It was as though these prophetic words were building a highway in the hearts of the people I grew up with in the Lord. My leader, Bill Johnson, and several of our elders began to view me through the prophetic words instead of through my occupation. They began encouraging me, empowering me and reminding me of my prophetic call. I really needed their approval because I was so unsure of myself, and I went through tough seasons of doubt and faithlessness. But their faith pulled me through the low days and kept me progressing in my divine destiny. I do not know where I would be today if it were not for Kathy and the leaders God put in my life, who trusted me before I deserved it.

Twenty more years passed, and in 1998 we left the business world and moved down from the mountains of Weaverville to join the staff at Bethel Church in Redding, California. Bill Johnson had become the senior leader there two years earlier. I could not have fathomed what was coming next. We left a small church of a couple hundred people who knew everything about me (my failures, mistakes and sins), and moved to a church of more than a thousand people who knew nothing about our personal lives. Immediately, Bill introduced me to Bethel Church as "a prophet" to the Body of Christ. We were not big on titles at Bethel, which is still true, but for some reason Bill decided to present me in a very different light to Bethel than the way I had been known in our little country

church. And as if that were not enough, Bill had been sharing the testimonies of my prophetic exploits with the Bethel
family before I arrived. (Thankfully, only the success stories.)
Suddenly, I was thrust into a world of incredible favor that I
found difficult to navigate.

My greatest challenge was learning how to work with the
pastoral staff at Bethel Church. I had been in the business
world all my life, and I had no formal theological training,
nor had I ever been to college. In contrast, most of the twenty
or so pastors at Bethel had graduated from seminary and had
years of ministry experience. Not only that, but I am not
sure any of them believed that I was a prophet or thought
that I was even qualified to be a pastor on staff. So while the
congregation embraced me with open arms, the staff was
cautious about my call.

Then one Sunday morning, something finally shifted. The
pastoral staff gathered in a small circle to pray before the
service began. Suddenly the Lord gave me a prophetic word
for Bill. He happened to be standing next to me, so I leaned
over and whispered in his ear that I had a word for him that
I wanted to share with him privately. But to my surprise, he
asked me to share it in the presence of the entire pastoral staff.

I was overwhelmed with anxiety, but I tried hard to hide
it. I gathered my thoughts and proclaimed, "The Lord will
raise all the money this morning for the prayer chapel that
we are building because of the divine favor He has placed on
Bill. God says this offering will be a public sign of the favor
Bill has gained in heaven because he chose to fear God rather
than fear the people when hundreds of them rejected the
outpouring of My Spirit on this house and left the church."

The service began a few minutes later. I was overcome with
anxiety again as the reality of the prophetic word settled over
my soul. My mind was so flooded with negative scenarios

that I could hardly think. I lay facedown on the floor, with my head under my chair, during the entire service. After worship, Bill got up to speak. Instead of teaching, he decided to share his vision for the prayer chapel and take an offering for the building project.

I was horrified! All I could think of was the embarrassment of getting the prophetic word wrong in front of the entire staff. After all, the cost of the prayer chapel was $237,000, and the largest offering in the history of our church had been about $30,000. To make matters worse, Bethel was in the midst of a serious financial crisis, but Bill felt as though we were supposed to build the prayer chapel "by faith."

When Bill finished sharing his vision for the chapel, he asked our people to pray and ask God if they should give, and if so, how much. Several minutes passed in intense silence as the people sought God in sincerity. Finally, Bill asked our congregation to come forward and put their offering on the steps of the stage. I could hear the footsteps of the people passing by me as I continued lying facedown on the floor. By now my shirt was soaked in sweat as fear gripped my soul.

When the traffic finally stopped, Bill asked our CPA, Steve, to get a calculator so that we could count the offering, while the people waited with expectation. Then he called up six of our staff members by name to help count the money. To my complete dismay, I was the sixth. I could not believe it. I crawled out on my hands and knees from underneath the chair and made my way to the stage, trembling like an alcoholic trying to detox. Money covered the front steps of the stage. I knelt down and scraped up a large pile of money and organized it by denomination, while separating the checks into another pile. I counted the hundreds and handed them to Steve, and then the fifties, and so on. The other five staff members were doing the same thing. Steve was subtotaling the money as we handed it to him.

Finally, all of the money was turned in, and Bill asked for a total. The calculator spit out a couple feet of paper as it compiled the subtotals, then it came to a heartless stop. Time seemed to stand still while Steve reviewed the tape. I was sitting on the steps, hanging my head, with my eyes closed. I could hear Bill and Steve conversing enthusiastically, then Bill excitedly announced the total over the PA system: "The total is $237,000.37!"

Of course, the people stood and cheered. I could hardly believe my ears. God had done it! He had raised all the money in one service. Honestly, as excited as I felt about building the prayer chapel, I was even more elated by the vindication of the prophetic declaration I had made.

For the next couple of years, this scene repeated itself over and over again. Many times, I would make a prophetic declaration to the staff and we would see it fulfilled. What I did not understand at the time was that God was promoting me among my peers. He was validating my call as a prophet to our leadership and to our church. When I look back at those days, I am humbled by God's mercy. I realize He chose to establish my calling by His grace.

The Process

I cannot count the number of times people have talked to me about their leaders not acknowledging their office as a prophet or prophetess. Typically, they have had some sort of prophetic word or personal experience in which "God commissioned them" as a prophet. They take this as a license to operate in the office of a prophet in their local church or ministry. What they fail to realize is that to have authority in any community, they must have the favor of God *and* the favor of man on their lives. That can be a process. Even Jesus Himself "kept increasing in wisdom and stature, and in favor with God and men" (Luke 2:52).

King David is a great example of this principle. God instructed Samuel the prophet to anoint a man king from the house of Jesse. The prophet went to Jesse's house and commanded all Jesse's sons to pass before him. When the last of seven sons stood before the prophet Samuel, he was bewildered, so he had a little talk with Jesse:

> But Samuel said to Jesse, "The LORD has not chosen these."
> And Samuel said to Jesse, "Are these all the children?" And
> he said, "There remains yet the youngest, and behold, he is
> tending the sheep." Then Samuel said to Jesse, "Send and
> bring him; for we will not sit down until he comes here."
>
> 1 Samuel 16:10–11

Jesse sent for his youngest son, David. When David arrived at the house, Samuel could finally carry out the Lord's instructions:

> And the LORD said, "Arise, anoint him; for this is he." Then
> Samuel took the horn of oil and anointed him in the midst
> of his brothers; and the Spirit of the LORD came mightily
> upon David from that day forward.
>
> Verses 12–13

Not only was David anointed king, but the next verse tells us, "Now the Spirit of the LORD departed from Saul, and an evil spirit from the LORD terrorized him" (verse 14).

If you did not know the biblical account, you probably would assume that David became king that day. But David did not become king for fourteen long years. In the meantime,

Israel lived with an unrighteous and insane king, Saul, until he finally died in battle. David had several opportunities to kill King Saul in those intervening years, but he refused to touch God's anointed. Although the Spirit of God had departed from Saul, he still remained anointed as king, a fact that David respected.

This in itself is a lesson to us all. It is not uncommon for God to anoint people to lead who are void of His Spirit. We will talk about this later in the book, but in the meantime, check out Romans 13:1–7, which starts out by saying, "Every person is to be in subjection to the governing authorities. For there is no authority except from God, and those which exist are established by God" (verse 1).

Finally, King Saul died in battle, and "the men of Judah came and there anointed David king over the house of Judah" (2 Samuel 2:4). Seven years later, "all the elders of Israel came to the king at Hebron, and King David made a covenant with them before the LORD at Hebron; then they anointed David king over Israel" (2 Samuel 5:3).

Note here that David was anointed as king three different times—once by God (through Samuel) and twice by men. The important point to grasp from this is that God may have called you as a prophet, but until the leaders in your metron or sphere of authority recognize, invite and empower you to wield influence and authority, you are only a prophet to yourself. I talk more about the important concept of metrons and how we influence or are influenced by the spiritual atmosphere around us in my book *Spirit Wars: Winning the Invisible Battle against Sin and the Enemy* (Chosen, 2012).

A prophet is definitely a leader, but you have probably heard what the renowned leadership expert John Maxwell says: "He who thinks he leads, but has no followers, is only taking a walk."

Favor with God, Not Man

What if you have favor with God, but you do not yet have favor with men? If you decide in that situation to take your "rightful place of authority," you will probably find yourself like the Old Testament character Joseph, who was thrown into a pit long before he was promoted to the palace. That could be you in the pit if you try to step into a place of authority before others are ready to acknowledge your call.

Joseph was the eleventh of twelve brothers, yet his father favored him above his siblings because he was the son of his old age. You may already know his story. (If not, you can read it in more detail in Genesis chapters 37 and 39–41.) Joseph's older brothers were extremely jealous of him because his father loved him more than the rest of them. One night Joseph had a dream from God in which he saw himself as a great leader ruling over his brothers. Instead of keeping the dream to himself and waiting for God to fulfill his call, he told his brothers about the dream. As you can imagine, this did not go over well with his older siblings. Then Joseph had another dream in which he was ruling over them and over his parents. Again, he told his family what he had dreamed. This further strained his relationship with his brothers, until they finally hated him so much that they threw him into a pit and sold him into slavery in Egypt.

As if that were not bad enough, Joseph rose to a trusted position in his Egyptian master's household and was then falsely accused of rape by his master's wife. At that point he was thrown into prison, with little hope of ever coming out again. But by divine providence and a series of miraculous circumstances, Joseph was called on to interpret a dream for Pharaoh and became ruler under Pharaoh of all Egypt.

It is an amazing story of divine promotion that we will talk about more in chapter 8, but personally, I think there were many paths Joseph could have taken to the palace. I do not believe he had to go through being sold into slavery and being put into prison to become the second-highest ruler of Egypt. I think God had determined Joseph's destination long before any of that. But Joseph's lack of wisdom and his arrogant attitude determined his rough pathway to promotion. In essence, he tried to take authority over his brothers before they were ready to acknowledge his right to lead.

We would do well to remember James 4:6: "God is opposed to the proud, but gives grace to the humble." You legitimately may be called to the office of a prophet or prophetess, but there is wisdom in waiting for God to grant you favor with men before demanding great authority and influence.

Favor with Man, Not God

On the other hand, certain people seem to have the uncanny ability to gain favor with others either without or long before they have favor with God. These people remind me of King David's son Absalom, who won the hearts of the people and usurped David's kingship, but all without the blessing of God. With an eye on position and power, Absalom did all he could to ingratiate himself with the people. Second Samuel 15:2–6 describes his political maneuvering:

> Absalom used to rise early and stand beside the way to the gate; and when any man had a suit to come to the king for judgment, Absalom would call to him and say, "From what city are you?" And he would say, "Your servant is from one of the tribes of Israel." Then Absalom would say to him,

"See, your claims are good and right, but no man listens to you on the part of the king." Moreover, Absalom would say, "Oh that one would appoint me judge in the land, then every man who has any suit or cause could come to me and I would give him justice." And when a man came near to prostrate himself before him, he would put out his hand and take hold of him and kiss him. In this manner Absalom dealt with all Israel who came to the king for judgment; so Absalom stole away the hearts of the men of Israel.

Absalom won over the hearts of the people with flattery, selfish affection and false promises. This was the political spirit at work in the hearts of the people, a divisive spirit that splinters any unity in its path. When Absalom thought he had enough favor with the men of Israel to overthrow his father, he made his move for the throne, which brought calamity on both his father and himself:

> Then a messenger came to David, saying, "The hearts of the men of Israel are with Absalom." David said to all his servants who were with him at Jerusalem, "Arise and let us flee, for otherwise none of us will escape from Absalom. Go in haste, or he will overtake us quickly and bring down calamity on us and strike the city with the edge of the sword."
>
> Verses 13–14

You can read the rest of the story in 2 Samuel chapters 15–18, but the net result was that Absalom lost his life in his attempt to take up authority without the favor of God on his efforts.

Self-promotion has become a way of life in the twenty-first century. Social networking has helped elevate image above reputation in our culture. It has created a platform from which people try to market themselves as trusted experts, when in fact, they may be deceivers like Absalom. Self-promotion is dangerous. I have watched the political spirit splinter and destroy countless congregations and devastate numerous families as some self-appointed prophet claws his or her way into prominence by stealing the hearts of people away from their leadership. The net result is never good.

Promotion and Protection

You may have heard the expression "greater levels, greater devils." This typically implies that when you are promoted spiritually, you should expect more intense warfare in your life. Yet what we sometimes fail to realize is that when God promotes us, He also protects us.

Think about what happens when a person gets promoted to the office of the president of the United States. That person is immediately assigned Secret Service protection. We would never think of promoting someone to the office of the president without protecting him or her. The protection comes with the position.

The challenge to our protection comes when we promote ourselves. Many people promote themselves beyond their protection, then they wonder why their lives are in a constant state of turmoil. Absalom, whom we just talked about, is one example.

Let me be clear—I am not saying that if God promotes you to the office of a prophet and your leaders recognize His call and commission you, then everything in your life will always be rosy. Warfare will still come your way, no doubt about it. But your level of protection will go up along with your promotion. I do want to point out, however, that if you attempt to scratch your way to the top yourself, that can and will leave you uncovered and underprotected.

Eager Beavers

Another challenge I see facing the Church comes from what I call "eager beavers." Many church leaders, feeling pressure to be in vogue with their peers, are eager beavers about promoting people too soon. A renewed awareness that apostles and prophets are such an important part of church government has caused many spiritual leaders to promote people unwisely and prematurely.

For example, I have watched leaders take the most prophetic person in their environment and commission that person as their "house prophet." This is a mistake on many levels. First of all, the gift of prophecy and the office of a prophet are two completely separate things. We will discuss the difference in more detail in chapter 5, but suffice to say here that just because someone gives accurate prophecies, that in no way means that the person is called to the office of a prophet.

Prematurely installing someone in the office of a prophet or prophetess is not only unhealthy for the person being promoted; it can also be a devastating experience for the congregation involved. As we emphasized when we talked about Joseph's story, between the promise and the palace there should always be a process that is natural and necessary. It is the process that prepares a person for promotion and develops in him or her the character it takes and the skills that are necessary to be successful in the palace, so to speak.

When we as leaders succumb to the pressure to stay spiritually current, we may promote people unwisely, before they have been through the process of preparation. That amounts to setting them up for failure. The spiritual pressure of a governmental office in the Body of Christ cannot be overemphasized. Although the weight of the fivefold ministry of apostles, prophets, evangelists, pastors and teachers is invisible, it is not intangible. I have watched many inexperienced and unprepared people—people who were genuinely called to a fivefold office but were commissioned prematurely—literally be destroyed by the very thing that they were destined to become. Many of them became disillusioned and left the ministry forever simply because their leaders did not use wisdom in preparing these precious people for their God-given purpose.

The apostle Paul emphasized this principle in his letter to Timothy, when he said in reference to leadership, "These men must also first be tested; then let them serve" (1 Timothy 3:10). He also warned Timothy, "Do not lay hands upon anyone too hastily and thereby share responsibility for the sins of others" (1 Timothy 5:22). Although Paul's subject in these passages is not the commissioning of prophets, the principles are still applicable. In fact, I would propose that these principles are even more important in their application to the fivefold ministry.

In the following chapters, we will look more closely at the process that is necessary for the preparation of those who are called to the office of a prophet or prophetess. Together, we will discover the culture that wise leaders must create to equip prophets and prophetesses for the challenges that lie ahead of them. We will cover many of the subjects that prophets and prophetesses need to master so that they can successfully wear this profound mantle and fulfill their divine mission. Ultimately, we want to see the office of the prophet and prophetess fully restored to the Church in a way that equips and prepares the saints to have a profound, positive impact on every realm of society.

2

NEW VERSUS
OLD TESTAMENT PROPHETS

In the twenty-first-century Church, there is much confusion over the office of the prophet and prophetess. Although I am excited to see the restoration of this important role, I am equally grieved over the misinformation, misunderstanding and overall misuse of this amazing and powerful gift to the Body of Christ (as well as to the world).

One of the greatest challenges we face in discerning the New Testament role of the prophet is that nearly all our prophetic models are in the Old Testament. Yet the great apostle Paul wrote, "For whatever was written in earlier times was written for our instruction" (Romans 15:4). We also know that our God is the same yesterday, today and forever. So the question becomes, how do the prophets of the Old Testament differ from the prophets of the New Testament—or do they differ?

Let's begin our investigation of that question by peering into the life of the prophet Elijah. The year is 885 BC. Ahab and Jezebel have again turned the heart of their nation away from the God of Abraham, Isaac and Jacob, to worship Baal. But suddenly a wild-eyed, revolutionary prophet named Elijah emerges out of the wilderness . . . a man who is vexed to the very core of his soul and who has had enough of Ahab and Jezebel.

Elijah is a student of the Torah, and therefore knows that serving other gods is cause enough to call for a curse on the land. He musters his prophetic unction, puts on his mantle and proclaims a drought in the land. The heavens obey the voice of the great prophet and refuse to release a single drop of rain on the nation. The drought causes a famine that lasts for three and a half dreadful years. The result is that all the livestock die, the orchards and fields become wastelands and water itself becomes so scarce that it turns Israel into a virtual desert. The people are literally starving to death in the streets to such an extent that some even turn to cannibalizing their own children to survive. Yet the prophet refuses to relent.

King Ahab institutes a massive nationwide manhunt to find the radical prophet and bring him to justice, but Elijah eludes him like the invisible man. Finally, the prophet steps out of obscurity and calls for a showdown at Mount Carmel with 450 prophets of Baal and 400 prophets of the Asherah, all of whom eat at Jezebel's table. The story is well documented in 1 Kings 18. The false prophets rave deep into the night, cutting themselves and making a scene, trying to get their gods to consume their sacrifice. After much drama and fanfare on their part, their offering remains untouched.

Finally, it is Elijah's turn. He prayed a simple prayer to the God of the universe, and all of a sudden a flood of fire crashes down from heaven, vaporizing the offering. It even "licked up the water" that Elijah poured on the sacrifice (verse 38).

Of course, the audience is stunned! Immediately, Elijah calls for the execution of the false prophets. As the people restrain them, Elijah slaughters all 850 false prophets, hacking them to death with his sword.

All this was meant to turn Israel back to God, but Ahaziah, the son of Ahab, became king over Israel in Samaria and walked in all the wicked ways of his father and mother. As a result, it would be years before Elijah's dream of a righteous nation would be realized.

Why Not Here, Why Not Now?

Now let's fast-forward about three thousand years, into the twenty-first century. Wickedness seems to go unchecked all around us. Murder, rape, immorality and idolatry run rampant in the streets of every major city around the world. Now the question is, what has become of the wild-eyed prophets like the ones who made the wicked kings of old tremble in their boots? Where are the radicals who caused famines and punished nations for their blatant sin and idol worship? Why don't the righteous drive the wicked out of their land, the way Joshua of old did when he destroyed all the terrible sinners with a massive genocide? Men, women and children all fell by the edge of the sword for not serving the God of Israel.

Why not incite a massive spiritual cleansing today and call down fire on abortion providers and homosexuals? Shouldn't adulterers and fornicators be stoned in our streets? Shouldn't liars and cheaters fall dead at the feet of our apostles? Surely nations that are filled with murder, export pornography, perform abortions and serve idols deserve to be destroyed, right? Don't we need the prophets to reestablish themselves as standard-bearers, holding the feet of societies around the globe to the fire of righteousness?

If God is the same yesterday, today and forever, then what is the holdup? Why not here, and why not now?

That is a fantastic question. In fact, many who read that last paragraph will feel inspired at the mere thought of judging the wicked. Others will rightly protest such harsh ideologies, believing instead that under the New Covenant, individuals should be shown mercy. Yet even some of those more merciful types will embrace the thought of prophetic judgments coming against cities and nations that practice wickedness.

Okay, let's think this through together. Is it not the presence of sin in individual's lives that ultimately leads to sin-infested societies? After all, it is not the buildings, roads or bridges that sin in a city. Neither do governments sin without people involved. It is those who govern and those they govern who sin. In other words, there is no such thing as a corrupt government without corrupt people in it. For example, laws can declare abortion legal, but it is people who have abortions and people who perform abortions. Where do you draw the line between individual responsibility and society as a whole?

The Twin Towers

To help us answer the question of whether cities and nations should be judged for sin, let's look at a real example of a fairly recent national crisis that many prophets viewed as a present-day judgment of God. September 11, 2001, the day the Twin Towers in New York City were destroyed, will forever be branded in the minds of Americans as a monument to murder. America woke up to the sounds of people screaming, many of them on fire as they exited the black smoke of a man-made hell. Many in the upper floors of the Twin Towers jumped to their death from those flaming infernos. Explosions could be heard in the background as buildings crumbled and thousands were trapped in would-be tombs. Weeping and wailing were heard for miles around as people wandered aimlessly through the streets, looking for their loved ones.

Deep sadness and fear blanketed the whole earth as the news of the terrorist tragedy spread. Everywhere, people cried out for mercy for those who were counted among the missing. People were glued to their TV sets, praying, hoping and believing that life would emerge from the rubble.

Although the "Prophets of Doom" had not previously prophesied this disaster, declarations of darkness began to emerge from what was supposed to be the "House of Hope" (the Church). Before we had time to ask ourselves why such a mindless act of horror would be perpetrated on the lives of so many innocent people, many "prophets of God" began to proclaim words of judgment for the sins of America. Their thesis was that God's hatred for sin had caused the 9-11 tragedy.

Can you imagine the grief that beset those who had lost loved ones? And then on top of that, they were confronted by "prophetic" words about a supposedly angry God who allegedly wanted to kill more people. These prophets of doom remind me of the words of Jesus when He said that in the last days lawlessness will abound and "the love of many will grow cold" (Matthew 24:12).

You would think that the prophets of doom would learn from their own mistakes. Remember that just two years before 9-11, several well-known prophets prophesied about an upcoming international famine. This became known around the world as the "Y2K bug." This bug was going to judge us for making our intellect a god. It was the perfect "God scheme," maintained these prophets, and the whole plan had been hidden from us by our foolish confidence in man's brilliance. It seemed that the Lord had blinded every computer nerd in the world, keeping them from discovering that we would all be starving over the lack of a digit.

What a way to go! There would be rioting in the streets. Businesses and governments would crumble. Some even predicted the Y2K bug would start the "mother of all wars." People streamed en masse to buy generators and guns, preparing themselves to protect their food supply "in the name of the Lord." But *nothing* happened! Not a thing!

I think what troubles me the most about the Y2K prophecies is that the prophets who proclaimed these judgments quickly removed their prophecies from their websites once nothing happened, and not one of them even bothered to apologize or admit they were wrong. To make matters worse, four years after the destruction of the Twin Towers, many of the same prophets refused to stop giving their judgmental proclamations. In 2005, they jumped on the bird flu bandwagon and started prophesying that this virus would plague the world and kill millions. Again, their dire predictions came to nothing. Yikes, people, get a clue!

Part of the challenge, though, is that once in a while these prophets of doom get one right. I guess even a broken watch is right twice a day.

The Salt of the Earth

Right about now you may be thinking, *Kris, I'm thoroughly confused. Are you saying that as prophets and prophetesses,*

44

*we have a responsibility to cleanse the land of wickedness
the way the prophets in the Old Testament did? Or are you
trying to tell us that God no longer judges and punishes evil
people who insist on infecting and infesting our nations with
sin, so we should be merciful?*

To answer these questions, we need to first get a grasp on
the New Covenant itself and then apply our understanding
to the office of a prophet. A good beginning point is to take
a look at the teachings of Jesus. He said, "You are the salt of
the earth; but if the salt has become tasteless, how can it be
made salty again? It is no longer good for anything, except to
be thrown out and trampled under foot by men" (Matthew
5:13). In Jesus' day, they did not have refrigerators in which
to store their food. Salt was the primary means by which
they preserved their meat and poultry. Through this analogy,
the Lord is teaching us that in the same way as salt preserves
food, believers are the element in society that preserves the
culture from the wrath of God and the destruction wrought
by evil forces.

Jesus went on to say that when salt becomes tasteless, it
is not good for anything except to be walked on by men. In
other words, the people of His day would taste the salt. If it
was no longer salty, but tasted like the food they were trying to
preserve, they knew it would not keep their food from spoiling.

It is important to remember that Jesus is not really talking
about preserving meat and poultry here; He is describing the
Body of Christ. What does it mean for believers to become
tasteless? It implies that we have ceased to be "salty," so now,
metaphorically speaking, we taste like the people we are supposed to be protecting. We have lost our ability to preserve
the world.

I would like to propose to you that we have become tasteless
when we prophesy against the very people we are supposed

to preserve. The words of the great prophet Ezekiel come to mind: "I searched for a man among them who would build up the wall and stand in the gap before Me for the land, so that I would not destroy it; but I found no one" (Ezekiel 22:30).

Jeremiah was commissioned with the same call of preservation on his life. God said, "Roam to and fro through the streets of Jerusalem, and look now and take note. And seek in her open squares, if you can find a man, if there is one who does justice, who seeks truth, then I will pardon her" (Jeremiah 5:1). Is it possible that the Lord is looking for prophets and prophetesses who will dare to position themselves between life and death, and who will have the courage to call for mercy on a world that does not deserve it? Isn't this what the Old Testament prophets Ezekiel and Jeremiah were compelled to do? Isn't this what the prophet Moses did with the wicked people in the wilderness? Read it for yourself:

> The LORD spoke to Moses, "Go down at once, for your people, whom you brought up from the land of Egypt, have corrupted themselves. They have quickly turned aside from the way which I commanded them. They have made for themselves a molten calf, and have worshiped it and have sacrificed to it and said, 'This is your god, O Israel, who brought you up from the land of Egypt!'" The LORD said to Moses, "I have seen this people, and behold, they are an obstinate people. Now then let Me alone, that My anger may burn against them and that I may destroy them; and I will make of you a great nation."
>
> Then Moses entreated the LORD his God, and said, "O LORD, why does Your anger burn against Your people whom You have brought out from the land of Egypt with great power and with a mighty hand? Why should the Egyptians speak, saying, 'With evil intent He brought them out to kill them in the mountains and to destroy them from the face of the earth'? Turn from Your burning anger and change Your

mind about doing harm to Your people. Remember Abraham, Isaac, and Israel, Your servants to whom You swore by Yourself, and said to them, 'I will multiply your descendants as the stars of the heavens, and all this land of which I have spoken I will give to your descendants, and they shall inherit it forever.'" So the LORD changed His mind about the harm which He said He would do to His people.

Exodus 32:7–14

This is a beautiful foretaste of the influence one prophet can have on the God of the universe. In this passage, God Himself pronounces a destructive prophecy against His Old Testament people, but a friend of God, who knows the heart of his Lord, steps in between God and the people and calls for mercy. The outcome? God *relents*. That's right—God changed His mind.

I have pondered these passages for years and have asked myself some hard questions. Was God saying, "Wow, Moses, thank you for reminding Me of the covenant that I made with Abraham, Isaac and Jacob. It had slipped My omniscient mind"? Maybe God is a rageaholic who sometimes loses His temper and just needs someone He trusts to calm Him down. But that is not the God I know.

So the question remains, why did God proclaim judgment against His people and then allow Moses to change His mind? Actually, I think it is because sometimes when God prophesies to us, He is testing our hearts rather than determining our destiny. Ezekiel 18:32 quotes God as saying, "I have no pleasure in the death of anyone who dies. . . . Therefore, repent and live." Moses knew God had such a heart toward His people, so Moses knew he had God by the heartstrings.

I believe that when God prophesied judgment and Moses called for mercy, God said to Himself, *I've found myself a leader!* If the Old Testament prophet, Moses, could call for mercy long before the blood of Christ was shed for the sins of the world, how much more authority do we have in the New Covenant to ask for mercy in the midst of people who deserve judgment?

We Are the Light

But wait! Not only is the Church preservation (salt), but we are also light. Jesus put it like this: "You are the light of the world. A city set on a hill cannot be hidden" (Matthew 5:14). We shed light on the nature of God and how God thinks and acts in the affairs of men. We are the revelation (light) of the Father and His love letter to the world. We "re-present" Christ to the lost. The lost look to us when they are trying to understand world events through the eyes of God. When we misrepresent our heavenly Father, the world gets a warped perspective of God.

At one point James and John decided to try out a doomsday prophecy on a Samaritan village because the people would not allow Jesus to pass through their city. These two asked Jesus if He wanted them to call down fire and consume the village, but He said to them, "You do not know what kind of spirit you are of; for the Son of Man did not come to destroy men's lives, but to save them" (Luke 9:55–56). I find it interesting that this is the same John who later exhorted us, "Beloved, do not believe every spirit, but test the spirits to see whether they are from God, because many false prophets have gone out into the world" (1 John 4:1). I imagine that through his experience of listening to the wrong spirit, he received the revelation that even Jesus' apostles could be influenced by hell.

One of the greatest tragedies in the world comes from negative prophetic voices who misrepresent God. Their declarations cause the lost to believe that our Father is an angry God looking for an opportunity to punish people. Jesus said, "If the light that is in you is darkness, how great is the darkness!" (Matthew 6:23). If we who are the light of the world are speaking and prophesying against people who are lost in darkness, how great is the darkness!

In the same way, when we represent God as someone who wants to destroy America because forty million babies have been aborted in our country, we perpetuate the very problem we are trying to cure. People are killing their babies because they do not know or understand the love of the Father. Does it make sense to tell such people that God is so angry because we are killing our young that He is going to kill all of us? Is our Father so single-dimensional in His being that He only has one response—getting angry—to anything man does wrong?

The Crossroads of Spiritual History

If all this is true, then why did the Old Testament prophets spend most of their time proclaiming judgments against people and nations? That is a great question, and the answer lies at the crossroads of history.

It all began at a famous dinner that Jesus held for His disciples before He was crucified. Of course, we call it "the Last Supper." This supper took place on a holiday the Jews call Passover, the day the Jews celebrated escaping the judgments of God in Egypt during the days of Moses. I am sure you remember the story of the plagues God brought about in Egypt because Pharaoh refused to let His people go. But God's judgment passed over the Israelites because they sprinkled the blood of a lamb over the doorway of each of their homes, as per Moses' instructions.

49

The Passover holiday actually originated as a prophetic act intended to prepare the world for the Lamb of God, whose blood would be applied to the doorposts of all our hearts. While the disciples were having dinner with Jesus, He explained that He was the Lamb of God who would die for the sins of the world. Jesus' death would fulfill the harsh Old Covenant, which said that a person who sins must die (see Ezekiel 18:20). At the crossroads in our spiritual history, Jesus' blood would inaugurate a New Covenant. Like the Passover in the days of Moses, this New Covenant would cause God to relate to the world through sacrificial blood—the blood of the Lamb. No longer would God relate to the world as He had related to Pharaoh and Egypt. Instead, Jesus became the door of destiny covered in the blood of a sinless lamb, which would cause the wrath of God to "pass over" the world.

Furthermore, Jesus' blood would create a new agreement between God and humankind, which would reconcile the world to our Creator once and for *all*. Luke records the Last Supper like this:

> When He had taken some bread and given thanks, He broke it and gave it to them, saying, "This is My body which is given for you; do this in remembrance of Me." And in the same way He took the cup after they had eaten, saying, "This cup which is poured out for you is the new covenant in My blood."
>
> Luke 22:19–20

Six hundred years before Christ came, Jeremiah prophesied that God was doing away with the Old Covenant and establishing a New Covenant with us. The author of the book of Hebrews captures his words so well:

> "For this is the covenant that I will make with the house of Israel after those days, says the LORD: I will put My laws

in their mind and write them on their hearts; and I will be their God, and they shall be My people. None of them shall teach his neighbor, and none his brother, saying, 'Know the LORD,' for all shall know Me, from the least of them to the greatest of them. For I will be merciful to their unrighteousness, and their sins and their lawless deeds I will remember no more."

In that He says, "A new covenant," He has made the first obsolete. Now what is becoming obsolete and growing old is ready to vanish away.

Hebrews 8:10–13 NKJV

Saying that the Old Covenant is obsolete and disappearing is like doing away with the Constitution of the United States and inaugurating an entirely new system of government. Every believer needs to understand the impact of this dramatic shift. The Old Testament Law no longer defines the way in which we connect to God or God relates to us. The old contract was fulfilled and became obsolete; therefore it is now irrelevant to the Kingdom.

Mutually Exclusive Relationships

It is imperative that we understand the difference between the Old and New Covenants so that we do not become, spiritually speaking, schizophrenic prophets or prophetesses. The Old and New Covenants are essentially two different relationships between humankind and God. These relationships are mutually exclusive, because the conditions under which these covenants were made were entirely opposite.

Let's explore these two relationships by starting with life under the Old Covenant. Jesus contrasted the Old and New Testament attitude of God when He taught,

You have heard that it was said, "You shall love your neighbor and hate your enemy." But I say to you, love your enemies and pray for those who persecute you, so that you may be sons of your Father who is in heaven; for He causes His sun to rise on the evil and the good, and sends rain on the righteous and the unrighteous.

Matthew 5:43–45

Jesus implied that they had heard it said that they should hate their enemies. Where do you think they had heard that? They got it from the Old Testament writers, because that was the attitude of our God under the Old Covenant. As a matter of fact, the Law of Moses made it clear that if you disobeyed God or served other gods, it would stop raining in your land (see Deuteronomy 28:24). Yet Jesus said something quite different in the quote we just read from Matthew 5. He said that God makes it rain on the righteous and the unrighteous.

Is the contrast between these two covenants coming to light for you yet? Read on, because there is much more for us to understand. Here are just a few more Scriptures that make God's attitude in the Old Testament crystal clear (and there are literally hundreds more of them):

The LORD your God will inflict all these curses on your enemies and on those who hate you, who persecuted you.

Deuteronomy 30:7

So now do not give your daughters to their sons nor take their daughters to your sons, and never seek their peace or their prosperity, that you may be strong and eat the good things of the land and leave it as an inheritance to your sons forever.

Ezra 9:12

Jehu the son of Hanani the seer went out to meet him and said to King Jehoshaphat, "Should you help the wicked and love those who hate the LORD and so bring wrath on yourself from the LORD?"

2 Chronicles 19:2

I hate the assembly of evildoers, and I will not sit with the wicked.

Psalm 26:5

I hate those who regard vain idols, but I trust in the Lord.

Psalm 31:6

The Israelites were commanded by Jehovah to go into the land of Canaan, kill everyone and take their property for themselves:

For it was of the LORD to harden their hearts, to meet Israel in battle in order that he might utterly destroy them, that they might receive no mercy, but that he might destroy them, just as the LORD had commanded Moses.

Joshua 11:20

Most of us probably have not thought through the Old Testament stories taught in children's church all around the world. Have you ever really thought about the story of David and Goliath, which is a tale about David killing a man who hated God? We celebrate the story, but we often forget that the big picture in the Old Testament is really about the divine mandate that was on the Israelites to kill all the Gentiles, who were considered enemies of God. Can you imagine going to church and having someone tell you that Jesus told him to kill everyone who had had an abortion or committed adultery? You would be on the phone with the police department in five seconds! But these are the kind of words that people in the Old Testament often heard from God.

Why was it that God was so tough on sinners under the Old Covenant? To answer this, we must understand the nature of a biblical covenant. First of all, a biblical covenant is unto death. It can be compared to the marriage vows between a man and a woman who, on their wedding day, repeat words something like "for better or worse, for richer or poorer, in sickness and in health, *until death do us part.*"

God made a covenant with humankind that included specific stipulations called the Law. The Old Covenant was based on the fact that God wanted to have a fatherly relationship with people and wanted to teach us His royal ways personally. But people insisted on living by rules that did not require that kind of relationship. Adam initiated this attitude in the Garden when, instead of learning righteousness through an ongoing relationship with God, he chose to acquire the knowledge of good and evil through eating the forbidden fruit.

Since that was the way people wanted it, so to speak, God subsequently made a covenant with humankind based on our desire to be righteous through our own self-efforts. That is where the Law came in. Yet God knew full well that our sinful state would prevent us from fulfilling the Law, so the Old Covenant's entire purpose was to help us see that we needed a relationship with God in order to live noble lives.

In that way, the Old Covenant prepared us for the New Covenant. But the challenge is that a covenant is terminated only by death. That was where Jesus' death on the cross came in. God had to die so that He could fulfill the requirements of the Law, create justice and establish the New Covenant, which ultimately extends mercy to millions who do not deserve it.

The Father's Heart

The merciless nature of the Old Covenant was not a revelation of the heart of God; it was a concession He had to make in order to breach the gap between the coldhearted, sinful nature of humankind and the righteousness inherent in sons and daughters of a royal King. Let's look at just a couple passages of Scripture that demonstrate this dysfunctional dynamic. Here is God's heart shared through Moses:

> Moses went up to God, and the LORD called to him from the mountain, saying, "Thus you shall say to the house of Jacob and tell the sons of Israel: 'You yourselves have seen what I did to the Egyptians, and how I bore you on eagles' wings, and brought you to Myself. Now then, if you will indeed obey My voice and keep My covenant, then you shall be My own possession among all the peoples, for all the earth is Mine; and you shall be to Me a kingdom of priests and a holy nation.' These are the words that you shall speak to the sons of Israel."
>
> Exodus 19:3–6

But look at the people's response to God's desire for that kind of relationship with them:

> All the people perceived the thunder and the lightning flashes and the sound of the trumpet and the mountain smoking; and when the people saw it, they trembled and stood at a distance. Then they said to Moses, "Speak to us yourself and we will listen; but let not God speak to us, or we will die."
>
> Exodus 20:18–19

Sadly, this attitude was expressed over and over throughout the entire Old Testament. This ultimately led to an entire population trying to "behave" without knowing God. But righteousness has always been the fruit of humble people having a close, personal relationship with a holy God. When the people asked to live by rules instead of relationship, they chose to labor for their own righteousness, which was a setup for failure. God had no choice but to judge them according to their works instead of according to His. The choice they made to attempt being justified by their own works led to an incredible debt of sin that mounted against the entire human race. All of humankind became powerless prisoners of sin serving life sentences in the slave camp of Satan.

God's Dilemma

How would God free the people He loved so much from their self-imposed bondage to the Law? How could He extend mercy to people who were guilty, without violating justice?

These questions make it clear that God had a challenge on His holy hands. He had to create justice for all of humankind so that He could extend mercy. Remember, God sits on the mercy seat, but the foundation of His throne is righteousness and justice (see Psalm 89:14; Hebrews 9:5). Allow me to tell you a tale that demonstrates God's predicament and His profound solution.

Late one foggy night, a violent man lurked in the streets of a sleepy, middle-class neighborhood. He peered at a beautiful home bordered by a wooded forest. The house was at the end of a long street darkened by a moonless sky and the absence of streetlights. Quietly he breached the front porch and took hold of the doorknob, picking the lock quickly. Clothed in black and wearing a ski mask, he crept through the front room, where a wedding dress lay on the couch. He shined his tiny flashlight down the hall and noticed a trail of shoes, pantyhose and underwear randomly littering the floor toward the master bedroom. He listened cautiously and determined that the newlyweds were sound asleep.

Slowly the masked intruder made his way to the dresser, where he spied the bride's beautiful wedding ring. As he reached out to steal the ring, the young bride woke up. Seeing the silhouette of the masked man beside her, she sat up, startled and confused, and began to scream. The robber covered her mouth, silencing her, then pulled out a knife. She fought back as her husband, still half asleep, jumped out of bed.

Desperate to save his wife, the young groom grabbed the intruder by the head and tried to dislodge the knife from his hand. Freeing herself, the bride kept screaming for help as her husband fought to subdue the attacker. Suddenly, she went silent. She fell limp onto the bed, blood pooling under her.

The robber wrestled his opponent to the floor, but Johnny, the husband, was able to dislodge the knife as they grappled on the floor. When the robber jumped up to flee, the desperate young man grabbed him from behind and pulled his ski mask off. Time seemed to stand still as the men glared at one another. Then the attacker sprinted toward the plate-glass window in the front room and jumped through, shattering it. Johnny turned back to help his new bride, but it was too late. Her lifeless body lay slumped across the bed.

It was months later that Johnny met his wife's murderer in court. His heart yearned for justice, both for his bride and for his own pain. But as the arraignment began, something about the proceedings seemed to go terribly wrong.

The judge turned to the defendant and said, "Henry Hamstead, your father and I were best friends and roommates in college. He used to brag about you when you were a little boy. I loved your dad. You're free to go!"

Outraged, Johnny jumped to his feet and began shouting in protest, "Your Honor, are you serious? That man killed my bride! He took away the love of my life. You can't just let him go free!"

"I'm in charge here," replied the judge, "and I choose to be merciful to this man."

"Yes, Your Honor, but aren't you also just?" Johnny demanded. "Doesn't justice matter to you? Or don't you have any integrity?"

While the judge hesitated over his dilemma, apparently waging war in his mind between justice and mercy, there was a sudden commotion in the courtroom as an elderly woman forced her way to the stand.

"Your Honor," the woman said through her tears, "Henry is my son, and I want to offer my life up for his. Take my life and let him go!"

The merciful judge turned to the magistrate and whispered in his ear. A few tense moments passed as the magistrate pulled a thick book marked with an *H* off a large bookcase that covered an entire wall. All the bookends were identified with letters of the alphabet, which were set in order on the shelves from *A* to *Z*. The magistrate put on his glasses and searched intently through the book. Finally he looked up, with grief on his face and proclaimed, "Mrs. Hamstead, I have found your name in the Book of Fugitives. You can't die for your son because you are also wanted for crimes punishable by death."

The courtroom was stunned as the woman cried out for mercy for her only son, pleading for his life.

"He was stealing to try to keep the bank from foreclosing on my house!" she wailed. "It was an accident. He didn't mean to kill the girl."

But the constable ushered her out of the courtroom in handcuffs.

A moment later, a young man in his thirties stood up in the back of the room.

"Your Honor!" he shouted, his voice quivering, "I will die for Henry!"

Shocked exclamations filled the courtroom.

"Your name?" the magistrate demanded.

"My name is Jacob," the young man replied.

His eyes met those of the magistrate and judge, and they stared intently at each other.

Suddenly the expressions on the faces of the judge and magistrate changed. They seemed to recognize something about the young man. The magistrate turned to the bookshelf and, finding the book marked *J*, he began to turn the pages nervously. The courtroom grew silent as the magistrate looked up in amazement.

"His name is *not* listed in the Book of Fugitives, Your Honor," the magistrate said. "I don't understand it! We are all guilty somehow. . . ."

Seeming to fear what this could mean for the brave young man who had offered himself up as a sacrifice for the murderer, the magistrate hung his head and stared at the floor, not wanting to meet Jacob's eyes.

"If he is not wanted for any crimes," the judge declared, "then no one can refuse to let this innocent man pay for the crimes of this guilty man."

Johnny jumped to his feet and protested again, "Your Honor, how can he take the killer's place when this man is guilty?"

"I had the magistrate check," the judge explained, "and even you and your wife are listed in the Book of Fugitives, wanted for crimes punishable by death. You are no less guilty than Henry here. Yet there is something different about this innocent man, Jacob, whose sacrifice will preserve the cause of justice. He is the only one I have ever met who can take the place of a guilty man, and justice will be served through the innocent so that mercy can be extended to the guilty."

This imaginative story illustrates how Jesus' death on the cross changed the conditions of all humankind standing before the Judge of heaven. Jesus was innocent; He never sinned and therefore deserved to live. But He took our place. All of us are fugitives, guilty of sins punishable by death. But the judgment that provoked the wrath of God was poured out on Jesus when He died for the sins of the world. With the cause of justice having been fulfilled by His Son's blood, the Judge of heaven is free to extend mercy to all sinners without being crooked or corrupt.

Paul said it best when he wrote that God "made Him who knew no sin to be sin on our behalf, so that we might become the righteousness of God in Him" (2 Corinthians 5:21). In the book of Romans, Paul wrote that Jesus "was delivered over because of our transgressions, and was raised because of our justification," and that, "having now been justified by His blood, we shall be saved from the wrath of God through Him" (Romans 4:25; 5:9). Jesus became sin so that we could become the righteousness of God in Christ.

The point here is not that God cannot judge sin in the life of a sinner; He is God and can do whatever He wants. The point is simply that He is not obligated to punish sin to create justice, because Jesus fulfilled justice on Calvary's cross. God now has the right to release everyone from sin without being an unjust judge.

Forcing Out the Old

Again, remember that for thousands of years, the Jews were told to detest, hate and destroy the Gentiles. When Jesus arrived on the scene with His "love evil men" doctrine, it was an incredible paradigm shift. A new grace was beginning to invade the Old Testament's world of judgment. Jesus went on to reinforce this dramatic contrast between the Old and

New Covenants when He said, "The Law and the Prophets were proclaimed until John; since that time the gospel of the kingdom of God has been preached, and everyone is forcing his way into it" (Luke 16:16). Matthew put it like this: "From the days of John the Baptist until now the Kingdom of heaven suffers violence, and violent men take it by force" (Matthew 11:12).

What does it mean for people to force their way violently into the Kingdom? That is another great question. Think of it this way: The Jews grew up reading the Law and the Prophets. And Jesus said, "Do not think that I came to abolish the Law or the Prophets; I did not come to abolish but to fulfill" (Matthew 5:17). The Law basically said, "You can't come into the Kingdom because you haven't kept the rules." Along those same lines, the role of the Old Testament prophet was to enforce the Law. That is why the prophets pronounce judgments against those who broke the Law. Thus the Law and the Old Testament prophets formed an impregnable wall, metaphorically speaking, around the Kingdom to keep people out.

But when Jesus was tortured and then crucified on the cross, He performed a violent act of grace. The cross became a battering ram that smashed through the iron bars of the Law and crashed through the bronze doors of prophetic judgments, allowing the unworthy (that would be us) into the Kingdom of God (see Isaiah 45:2). Consequently, we got into the Kingdom through His works and not our own, in a complete reversal of the former covenant.

As a matter of fact, the entire Old Testament's primary message was written to teach us that we could *not* keep the rules, and that we deserved to be punished and therefore needed a Savior. But the New Testament's message is that we are hidden in Christ—Jesus was crucified *as us*, not just for us, and His righteousness became ours.

The Messiah's Mandate

If you were to ask prophets and prophetesses, they would probably insist that it sounds overly bold to say we get to live in a realm of life in which we do not experience judgment, especially since judgment is a subject that looms large throughout both the Old and New Testaments. Let me clarify what I mean. Earlier in this chapter, we looked at judgment through the eyes of the Old Covenant. Now let's see what judgment looks like through the rose-colored glasses of the blood of Jesus.

We know that Jesus died for our sins, but what many of us do not realize is that He also died to deliver us from the judgment that those sins brought on us. This is the main point of the most famous verse in the Bible. You would be hard-pressed to find a Christian who could not quote John 3:16, but I hardly ever meet a believer who understands that this is a transitional Scripture—the passage on which all of history pivots:

> For God so loved the world that He gave His only begotten Son, that whoever believes in Him shall not perish, but have eternal life. For God did not send the Son into the world to judge the world, but that the world might be saved through Him.
>
> John 3:16–17

Jesus Himself said, "If anyone hears My sayings and does not keep them, I do not judge him; for I did not come to judge the world, but to save the world" (John 12:47). But perhaps the most powerful indication that Jesus did not come to judge the world began at what some theologians call the "Messiah's Mandate." It was Jesus' custom to speak in the synagogue on some Sabbath days. Though it is not mentioned in Scripture, tradition tells us that for hundreds of years, rabbis had set up in the synagogues a chair that was reserved for the Messiah. No one was ever allowed to sit in that chair. They believed that the Messiah would come one day and quote the Messiah's Mandate, and then He would sit down in the Messiah's chair.

One day, something profound took place in Nazareth. Jesus entered the synagogue and made His way to the Messiah's chair. You can imagine that the room grew suddenly and intensely quiet, as every eye in the place focused on Him. Jesus turned to the magistrate and was handed the scroll of Isaiah. He scrolled down to what we call chapter 61 of the book and began to quote the Messiah's Mandate. Dr. Luke records His words as follows:

> The Spirit of the Lord is upon Me, because He anointed Me to preach the gospel to the poor. He has sent Me to proclaim release to the captives, and recovery of sight to the blind, to set free those who are oppressed, to proclaim the favorable year of the Lord.
>
> Luke 4:18–19

The congregation stood there stunned as Jesus handed the scroll back to the magistrate and sat down in the Messiah's chair. But wait! Jesus also made a profound intentional omission as He quoted Isaiah 61. Look carefully at the original prophecy and see if the exclusion stands out to you:

> The Spirit of the Lord God is upon me, because the Lord has anointed me to bring good news to the afflicted; He has sent me to bind up the brokenhearted, to proclaim liberty to captives and freedom to prisoners; to proclaim the favorable year of the Lord *and the day of vengeance of our God.*
>
> Verses 1–2, emphasis added

Did you notice the New Testament version ends with "the favorable year of the LORD" and does not include the rest of the sentence, "the day of vengeance of our God"? The omission was intentional because Jesus' mission was not to bring vengeance, but salvation to the world. The "favorable year of the LORD" is a clear reference to the Jewish year of Jubilee. It came every fifty years, and it was the time when all debts were forgiven and all slaves were set free.

Jesus put it another way in the gospel of John: "Now judgment is upon this world; now the ruler of this world will be cast out" (John 12:31). Ever since the cross of Christ, the judgment that has been released is not against us—it is against the devil and his demons. Wow, think about the ramifications for us of living in a constant state of Jubilee, where we are free from judgment and we have power over the devil!

3

TWO DIFFERENT DISPENSATIONS

Let's take what we know about the New Covenant versus the Old Covenant and begin to apply it to the ministry of the prophet and prophetess. Remember what we learned in chapter 2? Jesus died to free us from sin, fulfill the Old Covenant agreement and inaugurate a new agreement. He fulfilled the Law *and* the Prophets when He died on the cross. He did not do away with the office of the prophet, but He did change the role and/or duty of the prophet. Paul clarified this change in the book of Ephesians when he wrote,

> He [Jesus] gave some as apostles, and some as prophets, and some as evangelists, and some as pastors and teachers, *for the equipping of the saints for the work of service,* to the building up of the body of Christ; *until* we all attain to the unity of the faith, and of the knowledge of the Son of God,

to a mature man, to the measure of the stature which belongs
to the fullness of Christ.

Ephesians 4:11–13, emphasis added

Although we will talk more about these verses later, right now I
want to highlight two things from this passage. First, Jesus continued the office of the prophet in the New Testament. Notice
that this office was given *until* the Body of Christ becomes "a
mature man." I do not think we are there yet, do you? Second,
we are beginning to see an entirely new prophetic role emerge
from these Scriptures. One of the New Testament prophet's job
descriptions, for example, is to equip the saints for ministry.

Hang in there with me for another minute as we look at
two more portions of Scripture and see how these verses affect New Testament prophets and prophetesses. Check out
what the apostle Paul wrote to the Corinthians:

> Therefore if anyone is in Christ, he is a new creature; the old
> things passed away; behold, new things have come. Now all
> these things are from God, who reconciled us to Himself
> through Christ *and gave us the ministry of reconciliation*,
> namely, that God was in Christ reconciling the world to Him-
> self, *not counting their trespasses against them*, and He has
> committed to us the word of reconciliation.
>
> 2 Corinthians 5:17–19, emphasis added

Did you notice anything in these passages that would relate
to the ministry of the New Testament prophet? How about
this for starters? All of us who are new creatures in Christ have
been given the ministry of reconciliation, *not* the ministry
of judgment that the prophets of the Old Testament were
given. What is the ministry of reconciliation? *Not counting
people's trespasses against them.* That passage all by itself
will destroy the ministry of a few prophets whom I know.

Now let's ask ourselves the million-dollar question: What would happen if you took an Old Testament prophet and transferred him to the New Testament side of the cross? Malachi answered that question four hundred years before Christ, when he wrote,

> Behold, I am going to send you Elijah the prophet before the coming of the great and terrible day of the LORD. He will restore the hearts of the fathers to their children and the hearts of the children to their fathers, so that I will not come and smite the land with a curse.
>
> Malachi 4:5–6

Notice that Elijah is going to return before the "great and terrible day of the LORD." In other words, he will return in the last days. And when Elijah returns, what will he be doing? He will be reconciling families.

Can you see the contrast between Elijah's roles in the Old versus the New Covenant? In the Old Covenant, he judged Israel and caused a three-and-a-half-year famine to punish them for their sins. He also called down fire and hacked 850 false prophets to death with a sword. But in the New Testament, he restores the hearts of family members to one another. That's right—Elijah was promoted from the ministry of judgment to the ministry of reconciliation through the cross of Christ. Hopefully, this revelation will transform all our ministries.

Ananias and Sapphira

For nearly a decade, I have been leading an annual school called the Bethel School of the Prophets. It seems as though every time I finish this portion of the teaching on the Old and New Covenant roles of the prophet, the room starts to buzz with whispers about Ananias and Sapphira. (See their story in Acts 5:1–10.) Finally, some poor soul will be unable to contain himself any longer, and he will dramatically raise his hand as if his question will destroy the entire theological foundation of my lecture. I have heard the question so many times that I know exactly what is coming: "Kris, if Jesus died for all our sins and therefore we are no longer under judgment, but under violent acts of grace, then why did God kill Ananias and Sapphira for lying?"

My dialogue with the students will then go something like this:

Me: "What did Ananias and Sapphira lie about?"

Student: "How much they sold their property for."

Me: "Who was questioning them?"

Student: "The apostle Peter."

Me: "Who is the most famous liar in the Bible? Isn't it Peter? And didn't Peter lie three times about knowing Jesus? What's more important to God, lying about how much you sold your property for or lying about knowing Jesus?"

Student: "I suppose lying about knowing Jesus."

Me: "Good point! So do you think that when Peter confronted Ananias, he had any idea that Ananias was going to die for lying? Don't you think Peter was as shocked as anyone else?"

Student: "I suppose so. But how about Sapphira? Peter must have known by then that she was going to die, right?"

Me: "Yes, but he still gave her a chance to come clean because he asked her the same question, 'How much did you sell the property for?' She chose to lie also."

Student: "Okay . . . and your point is?"

Me: "The book of Acts covers 28 years. Do you think that possibly, during those 28 years, any other believers lied to their leaders?"

Student: "Well, I suppose so."

Me: "In 28 years of New Testament history, there is no other recorded case of God taking a believer's life for any reason, including any sin. Now, my question is this: How many of you in this class have lied to someone since you've been saved?"

Students: "Well, yeah, I have. . . ." (They all raise their hands, of course.)

Me: "If God's normal mode of operation were to kill Christians who lied, how many of you would be in this class? Personally, I know you wouldn't have any instructors left!"

The students all laugh as they ponder my point, but their question brings up three important facts. First, as I mentioned before, God can take anyone home any time He wants to. (I do not believe Ananias and Sapphira went to hell.) God does not have to punish people for their sins so that He can create justice, because Jesus already provided justice on the cross.

Second, I think the most powerful point of Ananias and Sapphira's story is that while it is probable that hundreds of thousands of believers sinned over the 28 years covered by the book of Acts, God chose to take only two people home prematurely. That is called mercy!

My third and final point is that many leaders take an "exception" in the Scripture and make a culture out of it. That is not the pattern Scripture shows us, nor is it biblical. Think about this example: When Joshua conquered the Promised Land, God told him to kill *everyone* except Rahab the prostitute. Her life was spared. Joshua's cultural norm was to destroy all the Canaanites in the land, but Rahab was spared as an exception to the rule. Rahab's exception did not become the new cultural norm under the Old Covenant, though. For nearly twenty centuries after Rahab's salvation, the harsh rules of the Law still applied. The exception did not become the rule.

Today, however, I see many attempts to make exceptions the new rule. The idea of creating cultures from biblical exceptions was really driven home to me several years ago when I attended a "prophetic roundtable." About forty prophets sat together for three days, dialoging over their prophetic revelations. Frankly, it all felt pretty hopeless and judgmental to me.

On the second day, one of the most famous prophets came to the pulpit to bring us his prophetic word. "The Lord says that He is bringing back the days of Ananias and Sapphira!" he shouted.

The other prophets in the room clapped and yelled in agreement.

I waited for the room to quiet down, then I, too, shouted, *"Amen!"*

The rest of the prophets were stunned when they heard the "grace prophet" among them agree with that assertion. They all stared at me as if they were searching for an explanation.

I stood up and said, "Multiple thousands of believers sinned in the New Testament, yet God showed all of them mercy except two. So it's truly amazing that God would bring back the days of Ananias and Sapphira!"

I do not think the prophets of doom among us that day appreciated my insights. They seemed determined to create an entire culture out of a biblical exception.

The Last Days versus the Last Day

We have spent a long time contrasting the difference between the Old and New Covenants and unpacking the ramifications that these covenants have on the ministry of the prophet and prophetess. Now I want to talk about the two different dispensations that exist in the New Covenant. Misunderstanding the profound dynamics of these two dispensations can lead to seriously dysfunctional prophetic ministry.

The two distinct dispensations are called "the last days" and "the last day." Although the difference in their titles seems nearly undetectable, the ramifications of each of these dispensations are incredibly important.

The last days

Let me begin by explaining what I mean by "the last days." Review with me a familiar portion of Scripture from Acts 2. You have probably heard the story; the Holy Spirit has just fallen on 120 saints, and they are acting like people who are leaving a bar at two o'clock in the morning and have had too much to drink. The crowd is not sure what to think of them. Some are bewildered, while others tease the saints and make fun of them. The apostle Peter stands up under the anointing to clarify the situation:

> For these men are not drunk, as you suppose, for it is only the third hour of the day; but this is what was spoken of through the prophet Joel:
>
>> "And it shall be in the last days," God says,
>> "That I will pour forth of My Spirit on all mankind;
>> And your sons and your daughters shall prophesy,
>> And your young men shall see visions,
>> And your old men shall dream dreams;
>> Even on My bondslaves, both men and women,
>> I will in those days pour forth of My Spirit
>> And they shall prophesy.
>> And I will grant wonders in the sky above
>> And signs on the earth below,
>> Blood, and fire, and vapor of smoke.

71

SCHOOL OF THE PROPHETS

> The sun will be turned into darkness
> And the moon into blood,
> Before the great and glorious day of the LORD shall
> come.
> And it shall be that everyone who calls on the name
> of the LORD will be saved."
>
> Verses 15–21

I want to make a couple points from this passage that will help clarify "the last days" ministry of the New Testament prophet and prophetess. First, I would like to propose that we live in "the last days" that began at the cross, when the sun turned dark and the moon turned to blood.

Just as a side note, when Jesus died on the cross, the sun literally turned dark, and Jesus, who metaphorically speaking was the moon, turned to blood. The Scriptures often use such metaphors to communicate truth. For example, Joseph had that dream in which the sun and the moon and eleven stars bowed down to him. When his father heard the dream, he immediately responded, "Shall I and your mother and your brothers actually come to bow ourselves down before you to the ground?" (Genesis 37:10). Joseph did not say that his family would bow down to him. He simply recounted his dream to his father, and his father understood that the language of God is often full of symbols, like reading hieroglyphics. He knew that the sun, moon and stars referred to himself, his wife and his other sons.

When Jesus walked the earth, He often said that the words He spoke and the works He did were not His own, but were His Father's through Him. In other words, like the moon that has no light of its own but reflects the light of the sun, Jesus was the reflection of the heavenly Father working through Him. That is why I say that at the crucifixion, when the sun (the Father) turned dark, the moon (Jesus) turned to blood.

This began the dispensation the Scriptures call "the last days," which is also described as the "great and glorious day of the Lord" in Acts 2:20. Two amazing manifestations mark these last days. First, God will pour His Spirit out on all mankind (that means everyone), and second, "everyone who calls on the name of the Lord will be saved" (Acts 2:21).

"The last days" began at the crucifixion of Christ and will end when a new dispensation begins called "the last day," or "Judgment Day." There are thousands of years between "the last days" and "the last day." Many events take place somewhere on "the last days" dispensational timeline. Some of these occurrences are amazing, and some are very troubling. But God's intention for this first dispensation is to pour out His unreasonable, unimaginable, irrefutable, intense love and grace on the entire planet. His goal in this first dispensation is to reconcile the world to Himself by "not counting their trespasses against them" (2 Corinthians 5:19).

The last day

There is, however, a dispensational season change for all those who ignore the *days* of great grace. This second dispensation is called "the last day," or "Judgment Day," which is coming. The New Testament almost always refers to this dispensation as a single *day*, not plural *days*. We are currently in "the last days" plural, not "the last day" singular. Let's look at a few verses that talk about that singular "last day" that is on its way. Dr. Luke writes,

> Therefore having overlooked the times of ignorance, God is now declaring to men that all people everywhere should repent, because He has *fixed a day* in which He will judge the world in righteousness through a Man whom He has

appointed, having furnished proof to all men by raising Him from the dead.

Acts 17:30–31, emphasis added

The apostle Peter echoes Luke's words when he writes, "By His word the present heavens and earth are being reserved for fire, kept for the *day of judgment* and destruction of ungodly men" (2 Peter 3:7, emphasis added). Jude also repeats this theme: "Angels who did not keep their own domain, but abandoned their proper abode, He has kept in eternal bonds under darkness for the *judgment of the great day*" (Jude 6, emphasis added). The apostle Paul puts it this way:

> For I am conscious of nothing against myself, yet I am not by this acquitted; but the one who examines me is the Lord. Therefore do not go on *passing judgment before the time*, but wait until the Lord comes who will both bring to light the things hidden in the darkness and disclose the motives of men's hearts; and then each man's praise will come to him from God.
>
> *1 Corinthians 4:4–5, emphasis added*

I think Paul's message to the Corinthians is the most thought-provoking and insightful passage concerning the Day of Judgment because it does not concern itself with judging others, but rather with the way we judge ourselves. This portion of Scripture helps us understand that there really is no grace to accurately judge the hearts of people in this season we are in (this "last days" dispensation). As a matter of fact, Paul says that although he is unaware of anything wrong in himself, he could still be messed up and not know it! He goes on to explain that when the Day of Judgment comes, God will turn His spotlight on the hearts of men and reveal the inner courts of their souls. But until Judgment Day, we do not even have an accurate picture of what is going on in our own hearts, much less someone else's.

Let me draw some conclusions from these Scriptures and give some practical context to the office of the prophet and prophetess. The sons of Issachar were famous in the Bible for two things: They were men who understood the times, and they also had knowledge about what Israel should do in those times (see 1 Chronicles 12:32). In this chapter I have tried my best to help you understand the times we are in, because whatever you misunderstand you will mistreat. We have talked about prophecy under the Old Testament Covenant and under the New Testament Covenant, and we have talked about currently being in "the last days," but not yet "the last day." It is imperative—especially as a prophet or prophetess—that you do not superimpose a former covenant or a coming dispensation over your present role and thereby render yourself irrelevant, antiquated and ineffective in your ministry. The reality is that we live in the most exciting season in the history of the world, a time when God has chosen to pour out His Spirit on everyone in the human race. We have been released from the responsibility of judging people or nations, and we have been commissioned as prophets and prophetesses to extend the superior Kingdom everywhere we go.

Those of us who burn for justice can be reassured by the reality that there is a Judgment Day coming in which God will judge the wicked—but today is not that day. We should also remind ourselves that no matter what level of righteousness we have attained, we got access into the Kingdom by way of grace and not by way of any of our great works. It is therefore incumbent upon us as God's prophets and prophetesses to use our gifts to find the gold that lies buried in the dirt of people's lives. We must help people in the world understand that no matter what they have done, their heavenly Daddy loves them. It is easy to find sin in the lives of sinners or problems in the hearts of saints. In fact, you do not have to be prophetic to discover the profane things of life. But God has called prophets as His friends whom He can empower to unearth hidden treasures in secret places of darkness.

I have been teaching these principles concerning the prophetic ministry for years, and many times I have had people literally stand up and walk out of the room angry at me because they had patterned their ministry after some judgmental Old Testament prophet and were not willing to change it. Others have stood up and argued with me about their right and responsibility to bring about judgment against wicked people and/or nations. I have to say that there is something inherently wrong with us when we are so passionate about the ministry of judgment that we will fight for our right to punish people.

Good theology is so important. That is why I have taken so much time to help you process the Scriptures we have looked at accurately. James, the half brother of Jesus (who did not believe Jesus was the Christ until after His resurrection), penned these powerful words: "For judgment will be merciless to one who has shown no mercy; mercy triumphs over judgment" (James 2:13). Solomon, the wisest king in the history of the world, once wrote, "A man's discretion makes him slow to anger, and it is his glory to overlook a transgression" (Proverbs 19:11). What does it say about our self-righteous hearts when against those Scriptures, we insist on embracing the ministry of judgment? Have we not become like the elder brother instead of the father in the story of the prodigal son? When we refuse to be like the father and wait in the field of dreams for the plundered (see Luke 15:11–24), but instead we call for justice, have we not forgotten where the Father found us?

I have been called everything from an ear tickler to a false prophet simply because I refused to give people what they deserve. I have often been rejected by the so-called famous prophets because I have publicly renounced their judgmental prophecies. But I am convinced that many of them are just angry people looking for a place to vent their rage. That is not the last days' prophetic call. I love what Paul wrote to the Galatians: "Brethren, even if anyone is caught in any trespass, you who are spiritual, restore such a one in a spirit of gentleness; each one looking to yourself, so that you too will not be tempted" (Galatians 6:1).

My Prophetic Process

I honestly wish I could say that I learned to be a prophet of mercy through reading the Scriptures or through some powerful God encounter, but unfortunately that would not be true. The urgency I carry for this subject is because I have seen the damage caused not only by the self-commissioned prophets of judgment I mentioned, but by a prophet whom I know well—me. Before Kathy and I moved to Redding in 1998, we lived in a small town called Weaverville nestled in the Trinity Alps. Bill Johnson was senior pastor of our little church called Mountain Chapel for seventeen of those years. Danny Silk became the senior pastor of Mountain Chapel after Bill and Beni left to become the senior leaders of Bethel Church.

The first sermon Danny ever preached at Mountain Chapel was a message about offense and forgiveness in the Body of Christ. At the end of his message, he told the people that if they had something against anyone in the room, they needed to go to that person right then and reconcile. There were about two hundred people in church that morning. I looked around and saw nobody going to anyone. I thought, *What great relationships our people have with one another.* Then I looked behind me, and to my complete surprise, I saw a line of people extending out the front door of the building and leading up to my seat. They were all waiting to talk to me. One by one, they told me of the destruction I had caused in their lives over many years through my prophetic ministry.

It was painful as people recounted to me scenes that sounded like battle sequences from the movie *Braveheart*. But this was not a movie, nor was it a bad dream. No, it was my prophetic ministry. My prophetic words were almost always accurate, but they were also destructive, harsh and often given in the wrong spirit. I had made it my practice to call out people's sins, and it mattered not that I struggled with some of the same things. Not only were my words negative; I would often share them in church or in a group of people.

I had no idea how I was affecting the people I loved. That afternoon, somewhere around 3 p.m., I finally figured it out. I sat there for nearly three hours painfully and tearfully hearing each person's offense, until it finally occurred to me something was not right *in me*! I received what we affectionately call a "revelation bump." It took me months to process through all my pain, grief and regret. I sought the Lord earnestly through lots of sleepless nights and many tears. I relentlessly poured over the Scriptures like a thirsty man looking for water, determined to understand the heart of God for this wonderful call He had put on my life.

As days turned into weeks and weeks turned into months, I finally came to the conclusion that prophetic ministry, like every other ministry in the Kingdom, should be rooted in love. I came to understand that prophecy, as well as every other gift of the Spirit, is one of the love languages of God. Now I know the reason why 1 Corinthians 13—the most important exhortation on love in the entire Bible—is sandwiched between the main chapters on the gifts of the Spirit. That is what the supernatural ministry of the New Covenant is all about. As verse 8 of that love chapter says, "Love *never* fails."

4

PROPHETIC PERSPECTIVES

The image in the mirror reflected a skeleton-like figure, shoulders hunched, with thinning, brittle hair and yellowed, gaunt skin pulled tight against her face. As she stared at her reflection with hollow eyes, she saw that her clothing hung off her frame and her arms and legs were as thin as sticks. Self-defeating thoughts marched through her mind incessantly as she cowered before the mirror. She longed to be free from the bondage that enslaved her, but the lenses through which she viewed life clouded her vision continually, and all she could see was that she was overweight. She suffered from anorexia, and the lies that she believed affected the way she saw herself.

The way we see things is vital. In the Old Testament, prophets were sometimes referred to as "seers" because they were able to see things that were invisible to everyone else (see 1 Samuel 9:9). Their prophetic ministry was dependent on them seeing into the invisible and articulating what they perceived as the future reality. Although we seldom use the word *seer* to define New

Testament prophets and prophetesses, the term is still relevant. *Seer* actually describes how our gift often works and how we know the future; we literally "see it" before it happens.

Of course, it is important that the lens through which we view the future is clean, unblemished and undistorted. It is easy to understand that any kind of defect in a seer's lens could create a bias affecting his or her perspective of future events. In other words, a slight distortion of the lens could potentially have huge ramifications on a seer's prophecies. Think about the anorexic woman I just mentioned. This young woman viewed herself through a "lens of lies" that was severely distorted by deceit, which ultimately caused her to live a lie.

For seers (or anyone else, for that matter), core values are the lenses that determine *the way* we see life. Sometimes, if our core values are like a pair of glasses with smashed lenses, our view of life becomes so distorted that it is impossible to make out what is just ahead. Other times, our core values may be more like speaking with an accent. We all speak with an accent, though we often do not realize it until we are with someone who has an accent different from ours. (And of course, we all tend to think it is the other person who has the accent.) What most of us do not realize is that we also *see* with an accent. This visual accent is a kind of processing lens that shapes our view of our world, our view of God and our view of ourselves. We tend to see what we are *prepared* to see, what we are looking for and what we expect to see.

I used to believe that prophecies were supposed to come completely from God, but I no longer believe that is possible. Before you throw this book in the trash, let me explain. I certainly do not think that we should make up prophecies or add to a prophetic word the Lord has given us. But it is actually impossible to keep our "accent" out of our prophetic words. Our accent is created by our experience, our ethnic origin, our belief system and so on. Most often, we do not even perceive that we have accents because they are such a part of who we are. I would like to propose that God is so wise that He actually factors in our accent when He speaks through us so that we become part of the prophetic word. God specifically chooses people who see the world through a certain-colored lens to speak specifically to other people who need a prophetic word that is influenced by the flavor of the speaker's own life and love.

Consider how different the prophets Jeremiah, Daniel and Elijah were—a weeper, a wise man and a warrior. They were not broken (necessarily), but they each had their own unique flavor that made them effective in certain times and in particular realms.

Damaged Lenses

Metaphorically speaking, it is normal to have different-colored lenses and lives that have different flavors, but the challenge comes when prophets or prophetesses have lenses that are broken, smudged and/or crushed. Jesus put it like this: "So take care *how* you listen" (Luke 8:18, emphasis added). We often question what we hear, but we seldom question *how* we hear. This principle also applies to seeing. Many times we question what we see, but we hardly ever question *how* we see. The poor anorexic woman I first talked about saw a fat girl in the mirror because she did not question *how* she viewed her body. But since prophets and prophetesses are seers by calling, they must question how they see things. Otherwise, their distorted perspectives most certainly will affect and infect their future prophecies. Jesus explained it this way:

> The eye is the lamp of the body; so then if your eye is clear, your whole body will be full of light. But if your eye is *bad*,

SCHOOL OF THE PROPHETS

your whole body will be full of darkness. If then the light
that is in you is darkness, how great is the darkness!

Matthew 6:22–23, emphasis added

The Greek word for *bad* in the passage above is *poneros*. It
can mean "crimes" and "evil one," or it can mean "toilsome,
envious, evil, malignant, vicious, wicked and worthless." Core
values are like life coaches who interpret or reinterpret the
events of our world for us. Can you imagine having a life coach
named Worthless, Wicked or Envious who influences you day
and night and dictates how you see people, incidents and God
Himself? People who suffer with anorexia are a perfect example
of having a "bad lens," or having a worthless life coach (the
enemy) who twists the truth and victimizes innocent people.

A Bad Translator

Core values color and flavor our lives and give us an accent
that is beautiful, valuable and uniquely ours. But what we say
with our wonderful accent is determined by our different core
values. Our foundational core values become the principles
by which we decide what is real, true and right, as well as
what is fiction, falsehood and evil.

Let me illustrate with an experience I had in Mexico many
years ago. Bill Johnson and I did a crusade attended by a
couple thousand people. Bill preached the first two nights, and
I preached the final evening. We were seeing great fruit and
numerous miracles. I was excited to be speaking on the last
night so that I could bring the crusade to the ultimate climax.
But my Mexican interpreter had other ideas. My theme that
final night was that Christ will transform you from a sinner
to a saint. The struggle was that my interpreter was raised
in a church that only called famous *dead* people saints. He

had no grid through which to process believers who were still alive being named to sainthood, so he reinterpreted my message to agree with his core values.

Personally, I do not know a word of Spanish, so I was clueless that this was happening. I did notice, however, that the same people who were very responsive when Bill preached now seemed cold, stale and dead when they heard my message. I left the stage with my mind spinning.

What happened? I wondered to myself. I could not figure it out, and I felt so discouraged. I sat down in the front row with some of the bilingual Mexican pastors, and one of them rushed over to me and explained the situation. My Mexican translator had twisted my message and ultimately convinced the multitude that they were hopelessly bound to sin.

Foundational core values are like a translator. If they are clean, pure and right, you hear what was really being said through life and you perceive what is real. But if your interpreter has a prejudice, what you see and believe is real will actually be a perversion of the truth. Jesus said, "You will know the truth, and the truth will make you free" (John 8:32). The word *truth* here means "reality." Many prophetic people live in a "virtual reality"—it feels real and looks real, but it is not real. It is just an illusion.

Truth Is Reality

Unfortunately, many prophetic movements have gone off the rails of reality because they are being led by prophets and prophetesses who, frankly, live in a virtual reality. The message of these prophets is skewed because they have scratches on the lenses of their hearts. This problem can affect entire prophetic communities. When we have pain or brokenness in our hearts, it is like wearing dark lenses over our souls, lenses that obscure our prophetic insight and foresight. It is important that we understand the fact that we do not see the world the way it is; instead, we see the world the way we are. That is why we must listen to these words of King Solomon: "Keep your heart with all diligence, for out of it spring the issues of life" (Proverbs 4:23 NKJV).

When we have the mind of Christ, it gives us the amazing ability to process an incredible amount of internal and external stimuli and use it to interpret reality correctly. Having the mind of Christ radically changes how we see things. The scientific discovery about how our brain processes input from our optic nerves is a great example of this dynamic. The optic nerve is designed in a way that causes us to see everything upside down. But our brain receives other information from the rest of the body, and it makes a decision to reinterpret our reality by reversing the image we see to create what our mind believes is real. Our vision is an incredible process.

The same can be said of the process by which we filter what we see through the mind of Christ. What an incredibly brilliant process, unless something goes wrong and we *misinterpret* the facts in a way that leads us to become destructive prophets and prophetesses instead of constructive ones.

Trust Your Instruments

The question is, where do we start? How do we make sure that our hearts are not affected by a broken lens already? First, we must question our reality. Let me give you an example. Several years ago, I went to school to get my pilot's license. I never did finish, but I completed ground school. Our instructors beat it into our heads over and over not to trust our mind's perceptions when we were flying in storms, but instead to believe our instruments. There is a condition called *spatial disorientation* that, in severe weather, often causes pilots to feel as if their plane is upside down and rising, when in fact, it is actually the opposite. As a result of spatial disorientation, the pilot will turn his plane upside down and point it toward the ground, thinking he is leveling it out. This usually results in the plane crashing right into the ground. The pilot experienced a virtual reality—it looked real, felt real and seemed logical, but it was not real. Such pilots would be fine if they would just believe their instruments instead of trusting their instincts, but many do not.

Prophets and prophetesses are notoriously famous for trusting their instincts, too. Prophets are known for being intuitive and living from their "gut." This is a great quality, and it is often what sets us apart from other members of the Body of Christ. But it is also what gets us into the most trouble. We tend to fly by the seat of our pants and ignore our gauges.

Kingdom core values are like gauges in a plane; they help direct us in the affairs of our life and ministry. We install these gauges in our lives by touching the heart of the King and understanding His values for us as people and as prophets. If we are going to cultivate healthy prophetic communities, then it is incumbent upon us to learn how to develop the right gauges—Kingdom core values—and then use them as the instruments of our soul. This is the only way we are going to equip others to fly upright through the storms of life. When we gauge things by Kingdom core values, those who are flying with us, as well as those who are innocently grounded, will not become casualties of our prophetic ministry.

Clearing Log Jams

As prophets and prophetesses, we are the eyes of the Body of Christ. It is our responsibility and privilege to remove the slivers from the eyes of those whom we are called to serve. We are even commissioned to extract logs from the hearts of the hurting. But we simply cannot help other people when we are viewing the world through a worthless value system of our own (a "log" made of wood, hay or stubble), because it blinds us to the King's perspective. Jesus put it this way:

> Why do you look at the speck that is in your brother's eye, but do not notice the log that is in your own eye? Or how can you say to your brother, "Let me take the speck out of your eye," and behold, the log is in your own eye? You hypocrite, first take the log out of your own eye, and then you will see clearly to take the speck out of your brother's eye.
>
> Matthew 7:3–5

One of the ways I can discern if I have a log in my eye is by the way I view others. Most of the time, our opinions of others are more of a commentary on who we are than on who they are. For example, if I do not feel good about my performance at work, it is often easy to build a case against my co-workers who are high performers. My opinion of them is affected by my disappointment in myself, so I view them through the lens of jealousy. My assessment of them is really a commentary on my own heart and life.

This attitude of viewing others through a "log" is common among poor people, who often view wealthy people through eyes of envy. Because other people have something that they cannot seem to attain, they build a case against them. They say things like, "Those people must be tax evaders. They should be punished for stealing money. Money is evil, and those people are selfish. They've stepped on and used the rest of us to get rich."

This could be true of wealthy people in some cases, but to hold this kind of opinion about all wealthy people without knowing them personally is not only dumb; it is also unjust. And as a side note, I have never been hired by a poor person. People with money create jobs and generate a healthy economy. The *love* of money is evil, but money itself can be used for good by someone with the right core values.

Honestly, the only way to truly have the core values of the Kingdom is to be enlightened by the King. Paul put it this way:

> I pray that the eyes of your heart may be enlightened, so that you will know what is the hope of His calling, what are the riches of the glory of His inheritance in the saints, and what is the surpassing greatness of His power toward us who believe.
>
> Ephesians 1:18–19

The word *enlighten* in this passage is the Greek word *photizo*, which is where we get our word *photosynthesis*, meaning, "to build with light." God is building with light in us and through us. Jesus said, "I am the Light of the world," and then He turned to us and said, "You are the light of the world" (John 8:12; Matthew 5:14). Think about a world where prophets and prophetesses no longer build log cabins (metaphorically speaking), but instead enlighten people and help build cities of light where people can see the goodness of God.

In essence, Paul is saying that the key to building with light is having a worldview rooted in the revelation of eternal realities. This revelation creates the foundation for core values from three primary themes—the hope of His calling, the glorious riches of His inheritance in the saints and His power toward us who believe. All these realities have been made available to us through Christ.

This revelation of Christ will alter our reality so that we are accurately guided by Kingdom core values as we negotiate our way through the circumstances of life. Every prophet and prophetess must have his or her heart enlightened by the revelation of who God really is, who we are in Him and what He has commissioned us to accomplish through the power that raised Jesus from the dead.

Imagining a God Like Us

Let's explore how core values practically affect the ministry of prophets and prophetesses. Because core values affect the way we view God, the devil, the world and ourselves, they have a huge impact on our prophetic ministry. Core values interpret the way we relate events in life to God and which circumstances in life we attribute to God.

For example, if we believe that God is angry, we will interpret world events through that lens. Having "God is angry" scratches on our lens will affect *how* we see and hear. We will see and hear out of that paradigm. We will view natural disasters, terrorist attacks and famines as acts of God. Here are just a few examples of how "angry scratches" can affect our hearing and ultimately our ministry:

- We will give judgmental prophetic words.
- We will view natural disasters as God's way of punishing people for their sins.
- We will attribute sicknesses, especially diseases like AIDS, to God judging people.
- We will look for what is wrong in the world instead of what is right.
- We will have a Master-slave relationship with God.
- We will use the Old Testament prophets' mandate to prophesy judgment as punishment for sin as a model for our own ministry.

Since we were created in the image of God, we become like the God we imagine (image). If we imagine God as angry, then we will imitate His behavior. In other words, who God is *to us*, He will be *through us*. Having an angry God image creates harsh, judgmental and graceless prophets and prophetesses.

The other side of this same coin is that we tend to spiritualize our dysfunctions, meaning that we also create a god in our image. If I am an angry person, it makes me feel better to believe that God is angry, too. I will therefore find Scriptures to validate that being angry is spiritual.

It is not hard to understand how having wrong core values creates unhealthy ecosystems in us and through us. These dysfunctions perpetuate because they feed off one another. My view of God affects the way I see myself, and conversely, the way I view myself affects the way I see God.

If our lenses are clear, however, our hearts are pure and our core values are right. This dynamic perpetuates healthy ecosystems that promote wholesome prophetic communities. When Jesus said, "Blessed are the pure in heart, for they shall see God" (Matthew 5:8), He made it clear that it is only those who have flawless lenses who actually see God the way He really is.

We just looked at some examples of what prophetic ministry looks like when we view God as angry. Now let's explore the ramifications of having healthy core values. Here are the prophetic manifestations of seeing God as loving, affectionate and good:

- We will believe the best about people.
- We will extend mercy, grace and forgiveness to everyone.
- We will look for what is right in the world, not what is wrong.
- We will look for treasure in people.

- We will view death, sickness and disasters as the works of the devil, not as acts of God.
- We will feel empowered to minister life, healing and comfort to the world.

Defining Healthy Core Values

We have seen how powerfully core values affect our lives as people and as prophetesses and prophets. How do we develop in the right way the Kingdom core values that will affect who we are and what we say and do? To answer that question, we need to talk about these three things:

1. *Defining* healthy core values—we need to look at what they are, especially as they relate to the ministry of the prophet and prophetess.
2. *Assessing* our core values—we need to proactively assess our current core values and measure them against the truth.
3. *Assimilating* healthy core values—we need to assimilate Kingdom core values into our lives so that they become the lenses through which we live and minister.

Let's start with the definitions first. Here are several examples of healthy prophetic core values from the Scriptures. Every prophet and prophetess should embrace these Kingdom core values:

- Prophetic ministry involves looking for treasure. <u>The price that Jesus paid on the cross determined the value of the people He purchased</u>. God saw something good in us even when we were sinners. This core value teaches us that while it does not take a prophetic gift to see sin in sinners or junk in the lives of Christians, it *does* require the eyes of God to see broken people and in the midst of their brokenness, call them by a new name (the way Jesus saw Simon, whose name means "broken reed," and called him Simon *Peter*, which means "rock"). <u>True prophetic ministry involves looking for gold buried in the dirt of people's lives.</u> Our goal as prophets and prophetesses is to find treasure in the lives of sinners.

• Romans 3:23 says, "All have sinned and fall short of the glory of God." Jesus did not just die for our sins; He offered up His life because we *fell short of the glory of God*. This core value helps us keep in mind that the Holy Spirit convicts the world of sin, and we convict sinners of the glory they fell short of.

• Prophecy is for the common good, and the purpose of prophetic ministry is for edification, exhortation and consolation (see 1 Corinthians 12:7; 14:3). This core value trains us to realize why we do what we do as prophets and prophetesses. Edification means "to build up," exhortation means "to call near" and consolation means "to cheer up," so we are to build up, call near and cheer up those to whom we minister.

• Prophecy brings people into a revelation of the glory that God has assigned to them. This core value trains us to show people the glory that is possible in a relationship with God. The Bible says in 1 Corinthians 14:24–25, "But if all prophesy, and an unbeliever or an ungifted man enters, he is convicted by all, he is called to account by all; the secrets of his heart are disclosed; and so he will fall on his face and worship God, declaring that God is certainly among you." Paul tells us that prophecy reveals the secrets of unbelievers' hearts. Notice in this passage that the person who receives the prophetic word does not repent, but rather *falls down and worships God*. Most people know what is wrong with them, but they are unaware of the greatness that God has placed in their lives. This exposure brings conviction in their lives that they are living below the glorious standard that God has set for them.

- God wants to speak to us more than we want to listen. After all, how can God, who calls Himself "the Word," not want to talk to people? This core value creates an expectation in our hearts that we may hear Him at any moment.

- All things work in our favor when we serve God, no matter what the circumstances look like. This core value trains us to look for and focus on God's redemptive purposes rather than focusing on problems. As Romans 8:28 assures us, "We know that God causes all things to work together for good to those who love God, to those who are called according to His purpose."

- God loved us before we loved Him, and He never stops loving us. We never have to earn His love through good works. This core value trains us to focus on His love more than our lack, and to trust that we have an unlimited source of love to give every person we meet. "We love, because He first loved us" (1 John 4:19).

- Fear is not part of God's love and therefore should not be part of our supernatural ministry. This core value trains us to respond to, rather than react to, any kind of intimidation of the enemy. "There is no fear in love; but perfect love casts out fear, because fear involves punishment, and the one who fears is not perfected in love" (1 John 4:18).

- God has plans for our welfare and blessing. He has no plans for calamity in our lives. This core value trains us to see difficulties as opportunities for God to bless us and bring us more fully into His purposes for our lives. It also creates an expectation that God will bless us richly so we can be a blessing to others. It prevents us from coming under a poverty mindset. "'For I know the plans that I have for you,' declares the LORD, 'plans for welfare and not for calamity to give you a future and a hope'" (Jeremiah 29:11).

- We are a special, holy and royal people. This core value trains us to value others and ourselves as the precious possessions of God, for whom He sacrificed His only Son. It fosters a culture of honor in which we treat others as royalty because we are royalty. "But you are a *chosen race*, a *royal priesthood*, a *holy nation*, a people for *God's own possession*, so that you may proclaim the excellencies of Him who has called you out of darkness into His marvelous light" (1 Peter 2:9, emphasis added).

- We are to overcome and overpower anything evil that is against us. This core value prevents us from thinking of ourselves as victims of circumstance and frees us to think from a perspective in which nothing is impossible. It enables us to look for creative and extravagant solutions to problems. "But in all these things we overwhelmingly conquer through Him who loved us" (Romans 8:37).

- The devil is evil, and he is behind all the bad stuff in the world. Jesus is always good, and He does all the great things. We are called to destroy the works of the devil with our supernatural ministry. This core value keeps the lines of battle clearly drawn so that we are not directing *judgment* at people, but instead are bringing them the *justice* that Jesus purchased for them on the cross. "The Son of God appeared for this purpose, to destroy the works of the devil" (1 John 3:8). "The thief comes only to steal and kill and destroy; I came that they may have life, and have it abundantly" (John 10:10).

- We were born to rule through the power of the Kingdom and the love of God. This core value enables us to perceive the authorities and kingdoms of the world from an eternal perspective, so that our faith and intercession are founded firmly on the dominion of Christ. "Then the sovereignty, the dominion and the greatness of all the kingdoms under the whole heaven will be given to the people of the saints of the Highest One; His kingdom will be an everlasting kingdom, and all the dominions will serve and obey Him" (Daniel 7:27).

- We are God's friends, and He tells us His secrets. This core value reminds us that God wants us to live in intimacy with Him, far above obedience. He is calling us to move beyond slavery and co-reign with Christ. "No longer do I call you slaves, for the slave does not know what his master is doing; but I have called you friends, for all things that I have heard from My Father I have made known to you" (John 15:15).

- Signs and wonders follow all *believers*, not just a few special people. This core value trains every member of the Body of Christ to think of himself or herself as a carrier of the power of God and as being available for miraculous assignments. "These signs will accompany those who have believed: in My name they will cast out demons, they will speak with new tongues; they will pick up serpents, and if they drink any deadly poison, it will not hurt them; they will lay hands on the sick, and they will recover" (Mark 16:17–18).

- We have inherited the divine nature, and we grow in the fruit of the Spirit as we hang out with God. This core value trains us to embrace the journey of maturity as a process of yielding to the work of God within us and keeps us from adopting a striving mentality. "But the fruit of the Spirit is love, joy, peace, patience, kindness, goodness, faithfulness, gentleness, self-control; against such things there is no law" (Galatians 5:22–23). "For by these He has granted to us His precious and magnificent promises, so that by them you may become partakers of the divine nature, having escaped the corruption that is in the world by lust" (2 Peter 1:4).

These are just a few examples of the core values that we should carry into our prophetic ministry so that the power of the King and the love of the Kingdom flow together through us. I urge you to search the Scriptures with the help of the Holy Spirit to discover and develop your core values so that your life and prophetic ministry can be firmly founded on Christ's perspective.

Tainted by War

I want to move on to talking about how you discover or assess your core values, but first, let me briefly mention something that it is important you take note of as you assess your values. Note that prophets and prophetesses often have their core perspectives tainted by spiritual warfare that seeks to distract them. We see this in the life of Elijah. After destroying 850 false prophets and turning Israel back to God, he fears for his life because Jezebel threatens him. When the Lord meets him in a cave where he has spent the night, Elijah is feeling alone, suicidal, afraid and depressed. But it is all an irrational smoke screen. God reminds him that there are seven thousand other righteous people like himself in Israel, so he is not alone. (You can read the whole story in 1 Kings 19.)

It is not uncommon for prophetic people to war with this Jezebel spirit and other evil spirits. The great apostle John warned us about believing evil spirits and thereby becoming false prophets: "Beloved, do not believe every spirit, but test the spirits to see whether they are from God, because many false prophets have gone out into the world" (1 John 4:1).

I thought about writing an entire chapter on spiritual warfare here because prophets and prophetesses are so sensitive to it and so affected by it. But as I processed all the elements of spiritual warfare and the equipment we need to live in peace, it became obvious that it would take up not just one chapter, but an entire book. In fact, it did take up an entire book that I have already written titled *Spirit Wars: Winning the Invisible Battle against Sin and the Enemy* (Chosen, 2012). In that book, I shared my struggle with demons and my path to peace.

If you struggle at all with irrational fear, panic attacks, depression or any kind of mental or emotional torment, I highly recommend that you read *Spirit Wars* and perhaps join a *Spirit Wars* study group if one is available. (A curriculum kit is available that goes along with the book. It can be used in small groups or by individuals who need to study this area in more depth.) That book will give you the tools you need as a prophet or prophetess to live in freedom and to help others get free. It is much more effective to assess your core values when your assessment is not skewed by the distraction of spiritual warfare. In addition, getting free from bondage and the lies of the enemy will enable you to more effectively develop the Kingdom core values that provide a solid foundation for prophetic ministry.

Core Values Assessment Test

Now let's talk about my second question, How do we proactively assess our core values and measure them against the truth? Whenever I teach on the subject of core values, people ask me how they can determine if the lenses of their life are distorted or clear. I have contemplated this question for a long time and have developed a test that can be used as a tool to help determine this. The test is designed to give you an idea of how your core values might be affecting your life and ministry as a prophet or prophetess. For this test to be helpful, you must be as honest with yourself as you can. Answer the personal questions based on the way you are the *most* often, not based on your worst or best days.

Part 1

Scoring Key:

0 = Never   **1** = Seldom   **2** = Sometimes   **3** = Often   **4** = Very Often   **5** = Always

4   1. God is good.

3   2. Everyone is made in the image of God and is therefore a treasure.

5   3. Even sinners have good things in them.

5   4. I trust people until they prove they are not trustworthy.

4   5. It is my nature to look for good in every circumstance or person.

5   6. I do not hold grudges, and I forgive quickly.

3   7. It takes a lot to make me angry.

5   8. I enjoy being around people.

4   9. I do not take myself too seriously, and I can laugh at my mistakes.

5   10. I really like myself and expect people to like me also.

5   11. I celebrate other people's accomplishments.

4   12. I am not a jealous person.

5   13. I walk in a high level of confidence.

5   14. I enjoy being around very successful people.

6   15. In general, governments, corporations and organized institutions are trying to do the right thing.

4   16. The devil is defeated and therefore has no authority.

5   17. God has power over every circumstance and situation.

4   18. I do not worry, and I am not fearful.

4   19. Most wealthy people are generous.

4   20. I have no problem submitting to authority.

4   21. I am part of a church family.

5   22. In general, churches help connect people with God.

5 23. I am a positive, optimistic person.

3 24. I am not prejudiced against people groups or organizations.

4 25. Overall, I think the world is improving.

5 26. God is naturally good, and He favors us.

4 27. I do not listen to gossip or entertain bad thoughts about others.

5 28. I tend to get along well with everyone.

4 29. I do not struggle with sin issues in my life.

5 30. I do not spend time regretting the past.

4 31. I believe men and women are equally powerful, although they are distinctly different.

4 32. People love the prophetic ministry.

4 33. Prophets and prophetesses are called to encourage and confront the Body of Christ.

5 34. When God promotes us, He protects us.

5 35. Prophecy needs to be judged since prophets and prophetesses can make mistakes.

5 36. People have a right to ask me questions about my prophetic words.

5 37. It is important for prophets and prophetesses to be patient with people.

3 38. I feel people get me and understand me.

2 39. The prophetic office does not affect my personality.

5 40. My relationship with the Lord benefits the people I am in relationship with.

Please add up all the points from the part 1 questions above and total them on the line below. Then go on to answer the questions in part 2 of this core values assessment test.

201 **Total points for Part 1**

Part 2

Scoring Key:
0 = Never   **1** = Seldom   **2** = Sometimes   **3** = Often   **4** = Very Often   **5** = Always

_1_ 1. God is very angry.

_1_ 2. God hates sin and disciplines people who sin by making bad things happen to them.

_1_ 3. People have hearts that are basically wicked.

_0_ 4. There is nothing good in people who are not born again.

_3_ 5. I do not trust people until they prove themselves trustworthy.

_2_ 6. I am very discerning and look for ways that people might be trying to deceive me and/or others.

_2_ 7. I only forgive people if they repent and therefore deserve it.

_2_ 8. I carry a "righteous anger" in my soul because of the wickedness I see around me.

_2_ 9. I am reclusive and like being by myself.

_4_ 10. I am a sober-minded person who hates making mistakes.

_1_ 11. I struggle with low self-esteem.

_1_ 12. I have a hard time celebrating the victories of others.

_3_ 13. I find myself competing with others all the time.

_0_ 14. I do not have much confidence in myself.

_0_ 15. Being around very successful people makes me feel bad about myself.

_1_ 16. I think that most governments, corporations and organized institutions are corrupt.

_0_ 17. The devil rules the world.

_0_ 18. God has no control over the affairs of people.

_2_ 19. I feel as though I am always in a spiritual battle.

_3_ 20. Most wealthy people have no interest in God.

_3_ 21. I do not trust authority; most people in authority just want to control me.

_1_ 22. I am not part of a local church.

_0_ 23. Churches are religious institutions that take the place of God.

_0_ 24. I tend to be pessimistic.

_0_ 25. I think certain people groups or personality types are responsible for most of what is wrong in the world.

_0_ 26. The world is deteriorating.

_0_ 27. God has no patience with wicked people.

_1_ 28. I struggle with thinking negatively about others and talking badly about them.

_____ 29. I am not very easy to get along with.

_1_ 30. I have sin habits that seem to have power over me.

_1_ 31. I regret a lot of things about my past.

_2_ 32. It is normal for prophets and prophetesses to be rejected.

_0_ 33. Prophesying positively into people's lives is man pleasing and ear tickling.

_3_ 34. Greater levels, greater devils.

_2_ 35. My prophecies are always accurate.

_0_ 36. I get irritated with people who question my prophetic words.

_0_ 37. Prophets and prophetesses have a responsibility to judge sin.

_4_ 38. Women should submit to men.

_2_ 39. I feel misunderstood.

_3_ 40. It is normal for prophets to be abrupt and intense with others.

Please add up all the points from the part 2 questions *only* (do not add the points from part 1) and record your score on the line below.

_53_ **Total points for Part 2**

Final Grading Instructions

Now *subtract* your part 1 score from your part 2 score. This is your *Final Score*. (Your score may be a negative number.)

Part 1 Score <u>20 1</u>

minus

Part 2 Score <u>53</u>

Final Score _____

Now look at the graph below and mark your score with an X. This scoring system is designed to help you see how your core values are most likely affecting your personhood, prophetic office and ministry.

Analyzing Your Final Score

As you can imagine, this test (like most other tests) is highly subjective. It is in no way meant to act as the final word on your ability to function as a prophet or prophetess. A high positive score does not qualify you as a great leader any more than a low negative score disqualifies you. This assessment is simply a tool to help you analyze how your core values (the lenses of your life) are *most likely* affecting you both as a person and as a prophet or prophetess.

What does your final score mean? Let's begin with the two extremes. If you scored -200 (minus 200), you most likely have "scratches on your lenses" that are negatively affecting your perspectives on life. You have a hard time believing in people or empowering and developing them. You feel as though you are in a constant war with the devil that you are powerless to win. Life is a battlefield, and people are just pawns in an evil game of chess. Churches are religious organizations that are out to control people and shut down your ministry. This makes you highly cynical, which causes you to refuse to submit to anyone's authority. Your motto is "the Lord is my shepherd," and you therefore insist on following no man. You are convinced that governments, corporations and organized institutions have been infiltrated by evil; they are corrupt and cannot be trusted. You identify most with the stories of Jesus overturning the tables in the Temple and rebuking the Pharisees. Your negative approach to life often seems justified and validated by the fact that people and organizations reject you, warn others about you and "persecute you." The truth is that you probably need to get some help from a wise counselor and/or a person who has a great gift of discernment. The goal in meeting with someone for help would be to uncover the root issues that are skewing your core perspectives.

Now let's examine the other extreme. Let's say that you scored +200 (positive 200). Does that mean you are wearing clear lenses with no scratches and that you have perfect core values? The answer should be yes, but that may not necessarily be the case. There are some things you need to think through if you scored +200. You may be in danger of seeing God as the Big Sugar Daddy. If there are scratches on your lens, they may be preventing you from seeing the confrontational side of Jesus. You will need to ask yourself if all you see is Jesus kissing babies' foreheads and forgiving sinners. Ask yourself if you have a paradigm for the Lion side of the Son of God. Ask yourself if, possibly, you are a gullible person with too little discernment. In other words, a score of +200 should

Insufficient.

indicate that you have a healthy relationship with God, that you love yourself and others and that your view of life is accurate and undistorted. But it could also mean that you are not very self-aware or honest with yourself. Pray and ask the Holy Spirit to help you understand what your score indicates about you.

Let's be a little bit more realistic about these final scores, though. You probably did not land in the extremes of +200 or -200 on your test. How do you take your final score and use this test as a tool to determine your core values? The first thing you should do is go back over the test and examine your responses carefully. Ask yourself hard questions about the way you answered each question. The part 1 section of the test was designed for you to answer each question affirmatively with a score of 5, meaning *always*. The part 2 section of the test was designed for you to answer with a 0, meaning *never*. Wherever you answered differently than this, go back and ask yourself why.

Take note of whether any themes arose in your answers. For example, a theme of assuming the best in people, or a theme of thinking the devil has more authority than he has, or a theme of having self-esteem or self-confidence issues. Look at those themes specifically; they indicate overall patterns in your way of thinking. Did you have an experience that taught you a lie, or at least reinforced one in your life? Are there lingering disappointments in your heart or open wounds that need healing? Are you angry with God, yourself or someone else? Did the Church let you down, or did some leader try to kill your dreams? Did you grow up in a dysfunctional home, with the result that abuse and neglect play a big part in the way you view the world?

There are so many more questions you may need to ask yourself, but the goal is to search your soul with the assistance of the Holy Spirit until you arrive at a clear view of life. You may need to ask for help from a wise believer who can point out the blind spots in your heart and help you step into wholeness.

Assimilating Core Values

The final frontier of this chapter may be the least complex, yet the hardest to accomplish in our lives. How do we actually assimilate Kingdom core values into our hearts so that they become the lenses through which we live and minister? The challenge is that we often agree with the right core values, but we do not live them out. For example, the simple truth is that we can know John 3:16 backward and forward and sing "Jesus Loves Me" until we are purple, yet still not really believe in our *heart* of hearts that God loves us.

The real problem is that our hearts are really the throne of our core values, not our heads. So just because we can repeat a message does not mean we have become that message, or have assimilated it. The assessment test above is a great beginning place for us if we answer it honestly, because it helps mirror back to us what we really believe about God, others and ourselves. It can be a tool that helps us discover the disconnection between what we say we believe and the way we actually behave.

Because we cannot help someone who does not admit to having a problem, there cannot be change until a person has a revelation that something is wrong inside. We have to include ourselves in that; we will never change until we have a revelation that something is not right within us. It does not matter that everyone around us sees the problem. Until we "see" our problem, we cannot change.

They say, however, that adversity introduces a man to himself. That was certainly true in my life. Adversity introduced me to my real core values and revealed to me that what I thought I believed and what I really believed were not the same thing. I want to share with you a piece of my story that will help you understand my journey out of awful core values, values that led to decades of self-hatred. I will give you the condensed version here; you can read the complete story in my first book, *The Supernatural Ways of Royalty* (Destiny Image, 2006). My story begins with an experience I had with Nancy, who was my personal assistant. She entered my office one morning looking rather troubled. After we made small talk, I decided to ask her what was bothering her.

Nancy replied, "Sometimes you say things that hurt people's feelings. You're important to the people around you, and you seem completely unaware of how much people value what you think of them. You're devastating people with your words."

She went on to remind me of a comment I had made earlier. I thought I was being funny, but apparently I had actually made her my latest victim. I apologized to her, but honestly, I really did not think much of it. I went on with my day and pretty much forgot about our conversation.

That night I went to bed, fell asleep and had a dream. In the dream a voice kept repeating this Scripture: "Under three things the earth quakes, and under four, it cannot bear up: under a slave [pauper] when he becomes king . . ." (Proverbs 30:21–22). At three in the morning I woke up experiencing a deep sense of grief. I sat up against my headboard and tried to gather myself. I heard the Lord ask me a question: "Do you know why the earth cannot hold up under a pauper when he becomes a king?"

"No," I said, "but I have a feeling You're going to tell me."

The Lord responded, "A pauper is born into insignificance. As he grows up, he learns through life that he has no value and that his opinions don't really matter. Therefore, when he becomes a king, he is important to the world around him, but he still feels insignificant in the kingdom that lies within him. Subsequently, he doesn't watch his words or the way he carries himself. He ultimately destroys the very people that he is called to lead. You, my son, are a pauper who has become a king."

Through the wee hours of the morning, the Lord began to teach me about my identity in Christ. He took me to various Scriptures and showed me how important it is for His leaders to carry themselves as sons and daughters of the King.

When Nancy confronted me on the damage my humor was doing, it was more than just a wake-up call to the fact that I was hurting people. The greater revelation was that people valued what I had to say. I had always believed what my stepfathers had drilled into me—that people did not really care what *I* thought or said.

The realization that I had value began in me the process of uprooting the lies I had believed about myself and helped me find out who I actually was. God had called me His son, and I realized that my exchange with Nancy and the interaction I had with the Lord would be the first of many steps that God would use to lead me out of my prison and into His palace.

I had another encounter about a year later that became the next step in my journey out of low self-esteem. It began on a cold, wintery Sunday evening in December. I arrived at the church late, and as I opened the front door of the building, the wind nearly blew the door off its hinges. The prayer meeting was already well underway when I entered the room. About a hundred people were passionately praying, so I tried to slip in quietly so as not to disturb the meeting. Just as I cleared the door, Bill, our senior leader, greeted me and handed me something. He had the strangest grin on his face. I finally realized it was a check, but my disbelieving eyes struggled to communicate the amount with my brain. It was written out to me for *thirty thousand dollars*. I was so stunned that for several minutes I could hardly talk. I looked at the signature and realized that I did not even know the person who had given me the money.

Many days passed before I finally discovered the benevolent man's identity. He was new to our fellowship and had attended a class that I had taught earlier in the year. One night while he was praying, he felt the Lord tell him to give me a portion of his inheritance. I wrote him a card expressing my gratitude, but the strangest thing happened next. I completely avoided him for several months after he gave me that unbelievable gift. At first my avoidance was not so obvious, yet as time went on, it became more apparent. I would see him in a certain room in the church, and I would turn around and walk in the other direction. On one occasion, I ran to the men's restroom, wondering on the way if I was going to make it there on time. Just as I entered the bathroom, I noticed he was inside. His back was turned toward me and he had not seen me, so I ran out. I had to run all the way to the other side of the building to find another restroom. As I was racing around the building the realization struck, *Something is wrong with me!*

I really had no clue why I was behaving so strangely, and it troubled me. When I got into bed that night, I could not sleep. I kept looking at the clock, waiting for the day to dawn, tossing and turning and pondering why I was behaving so peculiarly. I could not get my poor behavior out of my head. My mind turned to other times over the years when I had had the same feelings toward other people who had shown me a lot of value. I thought about how many of those relationships I had sabotaged by not allowing people to love me. I became aware that I loved giving to people, but I never liked receiving from them.

Still, my behavior did not entirely make sense. Finally, in desperation I sought the Lord in prayer and asked, "Lord, do You know what's wrong with me?"

"Yes," He replied immediately.

"What is it?" I asked cautiously.

"Do you really want to know?" He asked.

That was a revealing question. I was fairly nervous about finding out what was wrong with me because I had been living in denial a long time. John Maxwell said, "People change when they hurt enough that they have to change; learn enough that they want to change; receive enough that they are able to change."[1] I recognized in that moment that I was hurting enough that I needed to change.

"Yes, I do, Lord," I replied.

Jesus told me, "The problem with you is that you don't love yourself enough to feel worthy of thirty thousand dollars. You're afraid that if that generous guy gets to know you, he'll be sorry he gave you the money. That's why you don't want him to get close to you."

My anxiety was growing deeper. I could no longer deny that I needed help. I asked, "Lord, what should I do?"

"Learn to love yourself as much as I love you," He replied. "When you do that, you will expect people to love you more as they get to know you better!"

I was stunned. I could not believe what lay at the root of my problem. Up until this point, the love I lacked for myself had never been exposed like that. I knew that others loved me,

1. John Maxwell, *Developing the Leader within You* (Nashville: Thomas Nelson, 1993), 63–64.

particularly my wife and kids, and I knew the Lord loved me. What I had not realized is that I did not love myself. My core value of low self-esteem, which was based on a deceptive lie, gave rise to hurtful behavior patterns that negatively affected my life and ministry. I needed to replace that damaging core value with a Kingdom core value based on the truth.

Heart versus Head

The great apostle Paul prayed a prayer that is a powerful depiction of what I want to communicate here about love and core values. He prayed,

> . . . that Christ may dwell in your hearts through faith; and that you, being rooted and grounded in love, may be able to comprehend with all the saints what is the breadth and length and height and depth, and to know the love of Christ which surpasses knowledge, that you may be filled up to all the fullness of God.
>
> Ephesians 3:17–19

Paul said he wanted us to "*know* the love of Christ which surpasses *knowledge*." He is making the point that there are some things you cannot fully understand until you have experienced them. The truth is that your heart can comprehend things that your head may never apprehend.

How does this relate to core values? Great core values begin in us when we are exposed to the truth, which subsequently reveals the lies we have been living out of. But we were never meant simply to remember or repeat truth; we were meant to *experience* it. Intellectual agreement with biblical concepts is the beginning of developing the right core values, yet until we work them out and walk them out in our lives, they remain philosophies or good ideas. For Kingdom core values to direct our lives as prophets and prophetesses, they must become our identity—who we are and *how* we think. Yes, it is true that core values determine *what* we think. But more importantly, they are the lenses through which we view the *what* in life, and subsequently they determine *how* we behave. There is no such thing as core values that do not affect our behavior.

The task at hand, then, is to assimilate truth until it molds the way we think, then ask ourselves how each of these core values makes us behave in the Kingdom. For example, every follower of Jesus believes in love, but as Heidi Baker says, "Love looks like something." It is incumbent upon us as prophets and prophetesses to discover the core values of the Kingdom and unearth the subsequent behaviors. For instance, what does honor look like when we minister to sinners, saints, enemies and those who disagree with us? How does honor behave in a conflict? How does honor affect the way we spend our money, our time and our strength?

Every truth is an invitation to a great adventure, and every Kingdom core value is an opportunity for a divine encounter. It is only when we embrace the truth and assimilate the right core values that we are enlightened. We can then see through clear lenses and live out of healthy behavior patterns. We can also minister truth and freedom to others as prophets and prophetesses in the New Covenant.

5

PROPHECY VERSUS PROPHETS

There is so much confusion between the office of the prophet or prophetess and the gift of prophecy. It is not uncommon for leaders to believe that a prophet is someone who gives accurate prophetic words. For that reason, I think it is prudent that before we continue to uncover the role of the prophet and prophetess, we first examine the difference between the office of the prophet and the gift of prophecy. Let's begin with the gift of prophecy. Here are some things the apostle Paul said about the gift of prophecy in his first letter to the Corinthians:

> Now there are varieties of gifts, but the same Spirit. And there are varieties of ministries, and the same Lord. There are varieties of effects, but the same God who works all things in all persons. But to each one is given the manifestation of the Spirit for the common good. For to one is given the word

of wisdom through the Spirit, and to another the word of knowledge according to the same Spirit; to another faith by the same Spirit, and to another gifts of healing by the one Spirit, and to another the effecting of miracles, and to another prophecy, and to another the distinguishing of spirits, to another various kinds of tongues, and to another the interpretation of tongues.

1 Corinthians 12:4–10

Pursue love, yet desire earnestly spiritual gifts, but especially that you may prophesy. For one who speaks in a tongue does not speak to men but to God; for no one understands, but in his spirit he speaks mysteries. But one who prophesies speaks to men for edification and exhortation and consolation. One who speaks in a tongue edifies himself; but one who prophesies edifies the church. Now I wish that you all spoke in tongues, but even more that you would prophesy; and greater is one who prophesies than one who speaks in tongues, unless he interprets, so that the church may receive edifying.

1 Corinthians 14:1–5

We can learn several things about the gift of prophecy from these passages. The first thing we learn from Paul's instruction is that the gift of prophecy is one of (at least) nine spiritual gifts of the Holy Spirit. The next thing we learn is that we are *all* exhorted to "desire earnestly" spiritual gifts. In other words, God commands every believer to pursue His gifts, but *especially* to pursue the gift of prophecy.

I propose that God wants to give us His gifts more than we could ever want them. As a matter of fact, the apostle Peter picks up this theme of every believer operating in the gift of prophecy when he quotes the prophet Joel in the book of Acts:

"And it shall be in the last days," God says, "that I will pour forth of My Spirit on all mankind; and your sons and your daughters shall prophesy, and your young men shall see visions, and your old men shall dream dreams; even on My bondslaves, both men and women, I will in those days pour forth of My Spirit and they shall prophesy."

Acts 2:17–18

Furthermore, the gift of prophecy is a *gift*; it is not an *award*. We did not do anything to earn it. The Greek word for gift is the word *charisma*, which means "favor which one receives without any merit of his own." We simply receive the gifts by asking the Holy Spirit for them.

Of course, this means that even very gifted people are not necessarily mature Christians. They may not even have good character. Consequently, the gifts of the Spirit do not validate someone's walk with God. Validation actually comes from the fruit of the Spirit that is developed in a person's life as he or she matures in Christ. The fruit of the Spirit is the evidence of our maturity in Christ. These fruits grow in us as we allow the Holy Spirit to work on us and not just flow through us (see Galatians 5:16–25).

I have been the senior prophet over Bethel Church since 1998. We have taken seriously the exhortation that God is pouring out His Spirit upon all flesh. We train everyone in supernatural ministry, from little children to the elderly. All our conference prophetic teams include two adults and a child. The children are uninhibited, and oftentimes they will give simple, yet more powerful prophetic words than the adults do. Even the toddlers in our church learn how to hear from God. (We will talk more specifically about equipping people in the prophetic ministry later on.)

The Gift of Prophecy's Purpose

Paul makes it very clear in 1 Corinthians 14:1–5 that the gift of prophecy has a triune purpose. It is for edification, exhortation and consolation.

- *Edification* means "to build up."
- *Exhortation* means "to call near."
- *Consolation* means "to cheer up."

Notice also that the *primary* purpose of the gift of prophecy is not to direct or correct the Body of Christ, but rather to encourage the Church. Paul uses some form of the words *edify* and *exhort* seven times in 1 Corinthians 14 alone.

It is unwise to allow people who are ministering in the gift of prophecy to speak negatively into the lives of others. The goal of the gift is to bring out the best in people. We are to mine the gold buried in the dirt of people's lives and find hidden treasures. If we see negative things in the life of a person to whom we are ministering, we need to ask the Holy Spirit to give us the answer to the problem we discern. Then we prophesy the *answer*, not the problem. This will result in people receiving grace (God's supernatural ability) to solve the problems they are stuck in.

For example, if we are ministering to someone who we discern is struggling with pornography, the Holy Spirit will often give us a prophetic word something like this: "God is calling you to a new level of purity and holiness." In this way, we have prophesied the answer without speaking about the problem, and we have released grace to break the bondage of pornography.

I am not suggesting that our goal is to discern a problem by the Spirit, come up with a solution and prophesy it. I am simply saying that when the Holy Spirit shows you a problem in someone's life, you should ask Him to give you a prophetic solution for the situation, then speak that word into the person's life.

New versus Old Revelation

While we are on the subject of contrasting the gift of prophecy with the office of the prophet and prophetess, I think it is important that we also contrast the prophetic ministry of the Old and New Testaments. We have already discussed the Old versus the New Testament dispensations, and we learned that the *primary* (though not exclusive) objective of Old Testament prophecy was judgment for sin, while New Testament prophetic ministry gives grace to people who do not deserve it. In this chapter, I want to compare the way in which prophetic insight was *received* in the Old Testament versus the way it is *perceived* in the New Testament. What we will discover is that New Testament people are supposed to process prophetic revelation from a completely different perspective.

Let me begin by explaining the way in which people from different dispensations acquired information from God. In the Old Testament, prophets *received* the word of the Lord. In the New Testament, prophets and prophetic people *perceive* the word of the Lord. In the Old Testament, the Spirit of God did not live inside people, nor was their human spirit connected to God. Our spirits were not given life until we were born again. When prophets in the Old Testament heard from God, it was quite an occasion because they were not the temples of the Holy Spirit. This principle is clearly portrayed in the words of Jesus when He said, "Truly I say to you, among

115

those born of women there has not arisen anyone greater than John the Baptist! Yet the one who is least in the kingdom of heaven is greater than he" (Matthew 11:11). In other words, John was great, but he was not living in the Kingdom and the Kingdom was not living in him.

All this affected the way in which the people of the Old Testament were instructed to receive and judge prophetic revelation. The only way people could judge Old Testament prophecy was to see if it came to pass, because the people who received the prophetic declarations were spiritually dead. They had no paradigm through which to process spiritual information. Through Moses, God gave the people instructions about how to relate to the prophets of the Old Testament:

> I will raise up a prophet from among their countrymen like you, and I will put My words in his mouth, and he shall speak to them all that I command him. It shall come about that whoever will not listen to My words which he shall speak in My name, I Myself will require it of him. But the prophet who speaks a word presumptuously in My name which I have not commanded him to speak, or which he speaks in the name of other gods, that prophet shall die. You may say in your heart, "How will we know the word which the LORD has not spoken?" When a prophet speaks in the name of the LORD, if the thing does not come about or come true, that is the thing, which the LORD has not spoken. The prophet has spoken it presumptuously.
>
> Deuteronomy 18:18–22

Notice that God said, "I will put my words in his mouth" (verse 18). It is pretty hard to get a word wrong if God literally puts His words in your mouth. The next thing we see from this passage is that God required the people to obey the voice of the prophet or die. That gave the prophets of the Old Testament some serious power and authority. From that, it is easy to understand why they killed Old Testament prophets who misled the people.

A Holy House for Two

In the New Testament dispensation, our spirit is alive and the Holy Spirit also lives inside us. Our body has actually become the home of two spirits—our spirit and the Holy Spirit. It is easy to get the Holy Spirit's words confused with our newly regenerated spirit's words because our spirit has taken on the divine nature (see 2 Peter 1:4). No longer is it only the Holy Spirit who wants to build people up in Christ; our spirit is now inherently good and very much wants to bless people. You can see how, in our zeal to help and encourage people, we can represent a word as a God idea when it is actually only a good idea. So in the New Testament, the believer who receives a prophetic word has as much responsibility to judge the word as the one who gave it, because both the giver and receiver have the same Holy Spirit living inside them.

In the Old Testament, prophets judged people, but in the New Testament, prophets judge prophecy. The apostle Paul put it this way: "Let two or three prophets speak, and let the others pass judgment" (1 Corinthians 14:29). Notice that the prophetic word is to be judged immediately. What exactly are we judging when we examine prophetic words? Obviously, the first thing we are called to determine is the source of the word. Is it from God's Spirit, the human spirit or a demonic spirit? And how can we judge a prophecy when it is about the future? The Holy Spirit who lives within us can discern the validity of the word and bear witness to our spirit, because He is supposed to be the source of all prophetic declarations.

What if we do get a word wrong? The fact that we are to judge the words means that sometimes "prophetic words" are not from God at all. It is also possible for part of a particular prophetic word to be right and part to be wrong. Because prophecy is made of three parts—revelation, interpretation and application—it is not too hard to get the revelation right, but then get the interpretation and/or the application wrong. It is easy to understand why Paul said, "Do not quench the Spirit; do not despise prophetic utterances. But examine everything carefully; hold fast to that which is good" (1 Thessalonians 5:19–21). The connotation here is to "eat the meat and spit out the bones."

The Office of the Prophet

When a person ministers in the gift of prophecy, the gift is the ability to prophesy. In other words, the prophetic words themselves are the gift. On the other hand, when people are called to the office of a prophet or prophetess, they themselves are the gift. Paul wrote to the church at Ephesus, "To each one of us grace was given according to the measure of Christ's gift. . . . He gave some as apostles, and some as prophets, and some as evangelists, and some as pastors and teachers" (Ephesians 4:7, 11). Notice how Paul said that Christ gave gifts to men, and that the gifts He gave are other people. A prophet or prophetess is Christ's gift to the Church. Their primary emphasis is not so much about what they do as it is about who they are.

Let me make a few more points that I think will help highlight the difference between the office of the prophet or prophetess and the gift of prophecy. There are basically three components to any mature ministry—our gifting, our calling and our anointing. Our gifting gives us our ability, our calling gives us our identity and our anointing gives us our purpose. Let's examine these three vital elements of fruitful ministry one at a time. I will describe each one individually as it relates to the office of the prophet and prophetess and the gift of prophecy.

Gifted

The gift of prophecy is a "gift." It is something we do and not something we are. We *have* the gift of prophecy, but *we are not* the gift of prophecy. Here is what the apostle Peter had to say about gifts: "As each one has received a special gift, employ it in serving one another as good stewards of the manifold grace of God" (1 Peter 4:10). Serving one another with the gifts Jesus has given us creates a beautiful community and a healthy culture.

The challenge is that if we receive our identity from our gift, it reduces us to a performance-based identity. Consequently, our self-esteem will be directly tied to something we do rather than who we actually are. This is one of the greatest challenges we have in leading prophetic people, and it is also one of the greatest temptations highly gifted people must navigate. When the motivation of our (prophetic) ministry moves from compassion and love to helping us feel valuable and worthwhile, the entire ministry becomes polluted, and the impact of our prophetic words is dramatically weakened.

I have watched this unhealthy dynamic take place in dozens of prophetic people's lives over the years. When people are getting their identity from the gift of prophecy, it is often hard to have a conversation with them without having them prophesy over you or tell you about something God shared with them. Frankly, people who insist on being spiritually hypervigilant annoy me. Their anointing is often undermined by their insecurity. It often helps to share these insights with them, but the truth is that I have never seen anyone overcome this unhealthy dynamic without first finding his or her true identity in Jesus. As prophets and prophetesses, it is incumbent upon us to help people find their God-given call so that they can operate in their gift in a way that builds a healthy culture in and around them.

Called

The second part of this tridimensional reality is our calling. The office of a prophet or prophetess is a calling, as is the rest of the fivefold ministry. With reference to his apostolic ministry Paul wrote, "Paul, *called* as an apostle of Jesus Christ by the will of God" (1 Corinthians 1:1, emphasis added). Paul was a gifted theologian, preacher and writer, but he was *called* as an apostle. It was not something he did; it was not his career. Being an apostle was part of his personhood and identity, so it affected the way he thought, felt and operated both internally and externally.

Much like the call to be an apostle, the office of prophet and prophetess is also a calling. Unlike the gift of prophecy, the calling of a prophet or prophetess on people's lives affects the way they think, the way they approach life, their inner world and often even the way they feel. This call can be on a person's life from birth or can come later on, when they are born again. Or they may not actually receive this call until many years after they receive Christ, as was the case in my life. (I shared that story with you in chapter 1.)

As prophets and prophetesses, it is important for us to understand this powerful dynamic in our lives, not just for the benefit of our theology or our ministry, but more importantly, because of the way it affects us personally. The impact of being called as a prophet or prophetess and not understanding these truths can lead to all kinds of dysfunction in us.

When someone grows up with a prophetic call on his or her life, it is not uncommon for that person to feel as if he or she is strange, weird or out of touch with reality. Just the simple fact that prophets and prophetesses see, hear and "feel" multidimensionally can make them feel crazy. This is especially true when the important people around them do not understand this dynamic and/or have no value for the prophetic perspective. In chapter 8 we will see from the life of Joseph what being raised in a prophetic family can be like, but suffice to say here that the prophetic call on a person's life will radically alter his or her reality.

Anointed

The third part of this tridimensional dynamic is the anointing. The anointing of the Holy Spirit upon us is what gives us purpose in life and ministry. The great prophet Isaiah gave us a perfect example of how the anointing affects us when he wrote, "The Spirit of the Lord GOD is upon me, because the LORD has anointed me to bring good news to the afflicted; He has sent me to bind up the brokenhearted, to proclaim liberty to captives and freedom to prisoners" (Isaiah 61:1).

Did you notice that the anointing was for a purpose? The anointing will always be associated with something to do—a purpose, a divine commissioning and/or a supernatural mission. I also want to point out here that the anointing is directly related to the Holy Spirit being "upon me." The Holy Spirit is in every believer, but He comes "upon" believers to instill them with purpose.

Paul said, "The gifts and the calling of God are irrevocable" (Romans 11:29). This means that God never retracts or takes back the gifts He has given us or the calling He has put on our lives. The anointing, however, is different. It ebbs and flows with our relationship with the Holy Spirit. We all know people who have a great call on their life and who are extremely gifted, yet have no motivation. This is often symptomatic of someone who has relationally lost touch with the Holy Spirit. The apostle John directly relates the anointing to abiding in Him:

> As for you, the *anointing* which you received from Him *abides* in you, and you have no need for anyone to teach you; but as His *anointing* teaches you about all things, and is true and is not a lie, and just as it has taught you, you *abide* in Him.
>
> Now, little children, *abide* in Him, so that when He appears, we may have confidence and not shrink away from Him in shame at His coming.
>
> 1 John 2:27–28, emphasis added

We really need to read the entire book of 1 John to get the full impact of John's revelation, especially since it includes an entire chapter about false prophets. But John's point here is clear: The anointing is directly related to abiding in relationship with God.

Gift versus Office Summary

What follows is a simple chart that summarizes the difference between the gift of prophecy and the office of the prophet and prophetess.

The Gift of Prophecy	The Office of Prophet/Prophetess
It is a gift of the Holy Spirit.	It is a gift of Christ.
It is something you do.	It is something you are.
Every believer is exhorted to seek to prophesy.	God chooses prophets; it is not our choice.
It is for edification, exhortation and comfort.	It is to direct, correct, warn, govern and equip.
Prophetic ability is the gift.	The prophet himself (or herself) is a gift.
The person is classified as a saint.	The person is called as part of the fivefold team.
The gift is for life.	The calling is for life.

There is much more to learn about the gift of prophecy and how it functions in the life of a believer. I have written extensively about prophecy in two other books, *Basic Training for the Prophetic Ministry* and *Developing a Supernatural Lifestyle* (both Destiny Image, 2007). If you are a prophet or prophetess but have had very little experience with leading people who have the gift of prophecy, you will want to do a more extensive study after finishing this book. In the pages here, my purpose is to teach and train prophets and prophetesses, so I have briefly provided an overview of the gift of prophecy as a means of clarifying the difference between prophecy and the office of the prophet or prophetess. You can delve deeper into this subject, though, in some of my other materials.

Warning, Correction and Judgments

It should be clear by now that the *gift* of prophecy is for edification, exhortation and comfort. On the other hand, someone who holds the office of a prophet or prophetess may sometimes have another purpose. Those with a prophetic office are sometimes called by God to warn and correct people. A great example of this role in the New Testament is the prophetic warning that the prophet Agabus gave to the apostles concerning a famine:

> Now at this time some prophets came down from Jerusalem to Antioch. One of them named Agabus stood up and began to indicate by the Spirit that there would certainly be a great famine all over the world. And this took place in the reign of Claudius. And in the proportion that any of the disciples had means, each of them determined to send a contribution for the relief of the brethren living in Judea.
>
> Acts 11:27–29

Agabus was a seasoned prophet who had a good relationship with the apostles, and he also had a reputation for giving accurate prophetic words. The first thing that comes to light in examining Agabus's prophecy is that his prophetic warning was not related to a consequence for sin. In other words, he did not call for a famine because of the sin of a certain nation or the failure of a particular person. It is hard to imagine an Old Testament prophet missing an opportunity to use a famine as a prophetic judgment against sinful people. Yet the New Testament prophet Agabus simply warned the people about a coming natural disaster. He did not call for anyone's repentance because he did not think the famine was punishment for sin.

There is an important difference between prophetic warnings and prophetic judgments. Since there are several definitions for the word *judgment* in the Bible, it is important to understand that the context the word appears in determines its definition. For example, we all have the right and responsibility to *judge* between right and wrong, or good and bad. When people do something bad, evil or wrong and we point it out to them, we have made a judgment. And often, when we call attention to someone's destructive shortfall in that way, they will respond with the old line, "Judge not, lest you be judged!" But they are wrongly using Jesus' words and taking them out of context, because knowing right from wrong was not the kind of judgment Jesus was referring to when He made that statement about judging not. He was talking about people who judge others in the sense that they want the person punished for wrongdoing. We do not have the right to ask God to punish people for their sins, since we ourselves have been forgiven of our sins. (We talked at length about that in chapter 3 when I compared the Old and New Testament dispensations.)

Here is a vital distinction we must understand: *Judgment* in the context of delivering a prophetic word is always directly related to being a consequence for someone's sin. *Warnings*, on the other hand, are entirely different. Warnings are derived from prophetic foresight into a future crisis. The goal of a prophetic warning is to divert a crisis or to save people from the consequences of the crisis.

You can call prophetic words *warnings*, but if they are in any way given to punish people who have sinned, or if sin is the cause of the crisis, then they are really prophetic judgments and not prophetic warnings. Warnings are not judgments, because God is not trying to punish people into purity or scare people into righteousness through them.

I have already made it clear earlier that as New Testament prophets, we do not have the ministry of judgment; we have the ministry of reconciliation. Yet God also has empowered His prophets and prophetesses to warn people of an upcoming crisis or disaster. People who desire to proclaim judgment on others often like to point out that Jesus judged three cities and several people. This is true, of course, but you are not Jesus, and neither am I.

"Wait a minute," you protest, "aren't we supposed to do the works of Jesus?"

The answer to that question is yes and no. Yes, we are supposed to love the unlovely, forgive the unforgivable, heal the sick, raise the dead and cast out demons. And no, we are not the Savior of the world, we did not create the universes, neither people nor angels should worship us, we do not have perfect discernment, we do not know people's hearts and we are *not* the Judge of the world.

Let me restate the obvious: Jesus is the Savior of the world, He is the creator of the universe, He never sinned, He knows the heart of every person and He is the Judge of the world, to whom all judgment is given. There are things that Jesus did, is doing and will do that we simply will never do. Jesus is the Judge, not you or me. Paul affirmed it like this: "I solemnly charge you in the presence of God and of Christ Jesus, who is to judge the living and the dead" (2 Timothy 4:1).

Warning cities

In one of my earlier books I shared a great story about a prophetic warning, and I think it bears repeating here. In 1976, a woman from Guatemala had a vision of great destruction coming to her country. She predicted that an earthquake would happen within the first four or five days of February, about four months from the day she had the vision. She submitted the prophetic vision to her leaders. They prayed about it and discerned that the vision was from God. In response, the church members humbled themselves before God and cried out for mercy. Then they slept outside for the first few days of February. The leaders told government officials about the vision, but the officials did not heed the warning.

At 3:02 a.m. on the morning of February 4, 1976, one of the deadliest earthquakes in recent history shook Guatemala, killing over 22,000 people and injuring about 74,000. Measuring 7.5 on the Richter scale, the quake destroyed entire cities, leaving one million people homeless. Remarkably, the churches that heeded the warning did not lose a single person.

Norman Parish, who was this prophetic woman's leader and the general director of Continental Missionary Crusade (CMC) based in Guatemala City, began a private relief program reported to be the largest in Latin American history. When the government saw the awesome job Norman's team was doing, they loaned him whatever he needed to help with the relief effort. They even gave him helicopters and assigned the national army to feed his relief teams.

Natural disasters

This is probably a good time to discuss the laws of nature and its workings. Earthquakes, tornadoes, famines and hurricanes are not necessarily acts of God or devices of the devil. Earthquakes, for example, are simply the sudden release of tectonic stress along a fault line. To relate every calamity to the spirit realm is simply ignorant and results in Christians losing credibility with anyone who has permission to think. I do understand that the spirit realm can and does have authority over the material realm, but God also created the laws of nature, which perpetuate without His intervention.

When we prophesy from a core value that God causes all natural disasters, we teach pre-Christians to blame God for everything that goes wrong in the world. Even insurance companies teach them the same thing by coining the phrase "acts of God" when referring to natural disasters that the companies will not insure. The Bible gives us a much different paradigm. As the apostle James said, "Every good thing given and every perfect gift is from above, coming down from the Father of lights, with whom there is no variation or shifting shadow" (James 1:17).

Sowing and Reaping

Years ago I was invited to a leadership event with several other apostles and prophets. We were there to process the condition of the world and help develop a strategic plan to transform the planet. During a lunch break, I had the privilege of sitting with several world leaders whom I had never met before. They were dialoging back and forth about the condition of the world and the ramifications of sin. One of them pointed out that people reap what they sow. From that statement on, the conversation shifted to the subject of judgment. I sat there quietly for nearly an hour while my new friends brought up several different ways that God judges people by causing them to reap what they sow.

I finally spoke up, saying, "Sowing and reaping is not judgment. Judgment requires a decision or a decree from the Judge to punish people for their sins. But when you reap the manifestation of your actions, that is called suffering the 'consequences' of *your own* devices, not a decision made by the Judge."

My friends did not seem too happy with my revelation, so I went on to give them a simple explanation.

"Gentlemen," I continued, "let's say that you warn little Johnny to not play in the street, but he doesn't listen to you and he gets hit by a car. He reaped what he sowed; in other words, there were consequences for the decision he made because he made a dangerous choice. But God didn't say, 'Boy, if you're not going to listen to Me, I'm going to send a car to run you over.' *No!* God did not make a decision at all. In fact, Johnny was the only one who made a decision in this scenario. So in what way did God judge Johnny? He didn't! The truth is that when we receive Jesus Christ, He forgives us of our sins and breaks the cycle of sowing and reaping in our lives. The blood of Jesus is so powerful that it actually keeps us from getting what we deserve. The truth is that Jesus wants to step in between the law of sowing and reaping, as we repent and follow Him." SOW JESUS!

My new friends were too committed to the judgments of God reaping destruction in our nations to agree with such a simple concept of grace and mercy. I love them all dearly, but they were wrong and I expressed that to them. Consequently, I was never invited back to their leadership seminars.

To sum it up, unlike someone with the gift of prophecy, those in the office of the prophet or prophetess have the right and responsibility to direct, correct and warn those who are under their authority. But I thank God that everything we do along those lines is based on love, not judgment. Love can make all the difference in someone's life.

Many years ago, the great prophet Bob Jones died and went to heaven. He told the story of standing before the throne of God, where Jesus asked him a question: "Did you learn to love well?" The next thing Bob knew, he was back in his body. Bob lived several more years and spent them learning how to love well. Last year he went home to be with Jesus. My life is a testimony to Bob's love. In 2009 my family and I went through the valley of the shadow of death. I called Bob numerous times in distress, and he answered my phone call every time. He constantly spoke life, peace and hope into my home. I do not know if we would be alive today if it were not for the love of God flowing through Bob Jones. It is imperative that as prophets and prophetesses, we learn how to love well.

6

THE ROLE OF THE PROPHET

When Ezekiel entered the valley of dry bones, the outlook was bleak. Death hung over the battlefield like a thick, dark cloud of gloom. Then suddenly, God rocked Ezekiel's world when He asked the prophet a ridiculous question: "Can these bones live?"

The great prophet staggered to comprehend the possible outcome of God's incredible inquiry. Finally he gathered himself and answered, "You know, Lord." The rest is history; a mighty army emerged from the valley of dry bones as Ezekiel prophesied life into that graveyard (see Ezekiel 37:1–10).

Like that bleak valley of dry bones, it seems as though our world is in complete disarray. Poverty, immorality and injustice are pelting our nations like a plague, and once again the prophets of God stand in the valley of the shadow of death. And once again God is asking us the same question: "Can these bones live?"

The future of our nations hangs in the balance as we ponder the answer to this profound question. Will we inspire mass despair, or will we equip a mighty army of light-bearers who will transform this deep darkness? The world waits in hopeful anticipation as the prophets and prophetesses of God stand in the valley of decision. My prayer is that God would once again equip us to see a mighty army rise from the dry bones of global despair, shining the light of hope into this desperate and dying world.

God's exhortation to Ezekiel to prophesy to the dry bones of a once-powerful army and restore them to their former glory was a shadow of things to come (see Hebrews 10:1). It was a foretaste of the most important role of the prophetic office—to breathe life into the dead, dusty, boney army of believers who once turned the world upside down, but who now have retreated into a life of powerless obscurity.

Like Ezekiel, believers are called to transcend the odds and transform history. The famous movie *Braveheart* reminds me of our call to courage. In one scene in the movie, a relatively small, tattered army of Scottish militia is gathered on a large battlefield. King Edward's English soldiers are assembled in orderly fashion on the opposite side of the field. The British soldiers are immaculately dressed and extremely well equipped, and they outnumber the Scottish army ten to one. The arrogant British generals shout across the battlefield to the Scottish rag-tag soldiers, "Surrender at once and we will spare your lives!"

On that note, William Wallace starts to ride across the field by himself toward the mighty English army. His right-hand man shouts to William in a heavy Scottish accent, "Where-ya going, man?"

Wallace yells back, "To pick a fight!"

The Scottish beat the British that day and eventually went on to win their freedom from the English. This feels like a scene right out of the gospels, where the Spirit of God led Jesus into the wilderness to be tempted by the devil. For forty days and nights, the Son of God refused to eat or drink anything. He looked broken, tattered and weak . . . like easy prey for a powerful devil.

The devil slithered into the wilderness on the fortieth day, brash and arrogant, ready to unleash his devious plot to destroy God's Messiah and take over the world. But what the devil did not realize was that the whole thing was a trap to lure him into the wilderness and defeat him on his own terms. Blow by blow they went at it all day, fighting from the pinnacle of the Temple to the highest mountain in the world. The devil barraged Jesus with every conceivable weapon in his arsenal, even using the Word of God against Him. But at the end of the day, the Son of God won. Jesus exited the wilderness in the "power of the Spirit," which launched Him into His public ministry of destroying the works of the devil (see Matthew 4:1–11; Luke 4:1–13).

Three and a half years later, Jesus and the devil would meet again for one final battle. Echoing Ezekiel's boneyard, this war would be fought at a place called Golgotha, which means "the skull." (Evidently, Satan must have missed Ezekiel's revelation that dead bones become a mighty army.) Satan finally managed to get Jesus nailed to a cross and buried in a grave. But unbeknownst to the devil, death could not hold Him, the grave could not keep Him and the devil could not defeat Him. The heavens thundered and the earth quaked as watching warriors and waiting witnesses gathered for three long days.

At last a huge boulder rolled away from a stone tomb, and Jesus emerged with a ring of keys (metaphorically speaking). "All authority has been given to Me in heaven and on earth," He proclaimed. "Go therefore and make disciples of *all* the nations" (Matthew 28:18–19, emphasis added).

The devil had once again fallen for the same tactic—underestimating a weakened Christ, a tattered army of unorthodox spiritual leaders and a bunch of disempowered women. But this time, his overconfident miscalculation would become his demise. If the devil knew what was going to happen to him at the cross, he would have killed everyone who was trying to kill Jesus!

You may be wondering, *Okay, Kris, what's your point? How does all that relate to your subject of the prophetic?*

Actually, I have four points for you. Keep these in mind and they will strengthen you in your ministry.

1. When everyone else sees a valley of dry bones, it is incumbent upon us as prophets and prophetesses to envision a mighty army and begin to procreate with God through prophetic declarations. As we see through Ezekiel's story, prophecy is not just telling the future. Oftentimes, God calls us to cause the future.

2. When the people of God feel defeated, depressed, powerless and outnumbered, it is the responsibility of the prophets of God to rise up and pick a fight against overwhelming odds. Prophets can see into the invisible realm, and they know that there are more who are for us than against us.

3. When the Body of Christ encounters demonic forces in the dark night of the soul and believers feel weak, hungry and fragile, it is the prophets and prophetesses of God who can see past the plots of the enemy and envision the battle plans of the angel armies. This gives us authority to release declarations of hope in the midst of a house of horrors, which in turn ensnares principalities and disarms and imprisons them in their own demonic devices.

4. Finally, when the mourners saw a crucified body and the soldiers were counting their coins, and when Pilate had

long since washed his hands of the whole mess, it was time to keep in mind that the prophets of God thousands of years earlier had already predicted an empty tomb.

Having said all that, I see a trend in the Body of Christ among some prophets that is both alarming and destructive. Some prophetic people are taking a mighty army and turning them into a valley of dry bones. They are literally talking people to death. They insist on seeing dry bones (tough circumstances, sin issues, etc.) and giving a detailed commentary on the negative conditions of life and/or society and then calling it a prophecy. But prophecy is often seeing the negative situations of life through the eyes of God and then calling things that are not as though they are.

Metaphorically speaking, seeing a valley of dry bones and using your prophetic gift to get the name of each skeleton and give the details of its death may wow people, but it will not transform those dry bones back into a mighty army. Remember, life and death are in the tongue (see Proverbs 18:21).

Building with Words

In the Old Testament, the Babylonians destroyed Israel and took all the people into captivity. Jeremiah the prophet began to proclaim that Israel would be in captivity for seventy years, then finally be released back into their land to rebuild the country (see Jeremiah 29:10–14). Daniel survived the attack and became a POW in Babylon. He served four different kings over the next seventy years. For all those years, Daniel opened his window toward Jerusalem and prayed three times a day for the fulfillment of Jeremiah's revelation—the release of the Israelites.

In the seventieth year Daniel was serving King Cyrus, whom

Isaiah had named as the king who would release the people of God back to their homeland (see Isaiah 45:1). Through a series of circumstances, Cyrus made a decree that the Israelites could go home, but there was even more. The Persian king also decided to fund the entire rebuilding of the Temple from the king's own treasury. It was the most expensive single rebuilding project in the history of the world. You can read about it in the books of Ezra and Nehemiah. It is a wonderful story of great faith, perseverance and hard work.

Ezra the priest and scribe was most likely the chief architect in the rebuilding of the Temple because he was well acquainted with the biblical account of the original Temple of Solomon. Here is Ezra's account of the project's beginning:

> Zerubbabel the son of Shealtiel and Jeshua the son of Jozadak and the rest of their brothers the priests and the Levites, and all who came from the captivity to Jerusalem, began the work and appointed the Levites from twenty years and older to oversee the work of the house of the LORD.
>
> Ezra 3:8

Ezra went on to say that "the prophets of God were with them supporting them" (Ezra 5:2). He also added later,

> The elders of the Jews were successful in building through the prophesying of Haggai the prophet and Zechariah the son of Iddo. And they finished building according to the command of the God of Israel and the decree of Cyrus, Darius, and Artaxerxes king of Persia.
>
> Ezra 6:14

Did you notice the elements of success in this project? There were Levites, scribes, a priest and a couple of godly project managers, Zerubbabel and Jeshua, who were overseeing the building project along with the elders of Israel.

There were the people who were freed from captivity, who became the primary laborers. There were also three kings, Cyrus, Darius and Artaxerxes, who made decrees in favor of the project. But Ezra said that the project actually succeeded because of the prophesying of two prophets, Haggai and Zechariah. That's right—laborers, project managers, kings, money, power and even spiritual advisers were all an important part of rebuilding the Temple, *but* when push came to shove, it was the prophets of God who made the project work.

Prophets Are Builders

It should not surprise us that the prophets Haggai and Zechariah were helping rebuild the great Temple. As we have already discussed, the heart of prophecy is to edify the Church. This dynamic was alive in the early Church. Luke gives this account of the prophets' role among first-century believers: "Judas and Silas, also being prophets themselves, encouraged and strengthened the brethren with a lengthy message" (Acts 15:32). The apostle Paul put it this way: "One who speaks in a tongue edifies himself; but one who prophesies edifies the church" (1 Corinthians 14:4).

The Greek word for *edify* in this passage is *oikodomeo*, which means "to build a house." Speaking of that, let me take a little detour here. Did you notice that speaking in tongues builds your own house? When we pray in tongues, we become our own contractors working on the temple of the Holy Spirit. Now, that is amazing! Yet when we prophesy, we help build homes for others. Just imagine what is happening in the lives of people as we prophesy God's destiny into their soul. As prophets and prophetesses, we speak into the hearts of people, and our words are becoming living stones building beautiful castles that the Holy Spirit inhabits. We also build fortresses that protect people from the storms of life.

As prophets, we are builders sent from God and commissioned to build great edifices for the Kingdom of God. We build with light, infused with love. We enlighten people. We build cities on hills, which cannot be hidden. That is who we are as God's prophets and prophetesses. We are here to build lighthouses in the darkest places of the planet to guide people to our great King.

This is our call—that we arise in this darkness, as in the days of Ezra, and build something so beautiful and so incredibly profound that the kings of the earth come to seek the wisdom of the ages from these houses of hope. It is our duty as prophets and prophetesses to transform the Church of the living God from destruction sites to construction sites, places where people come to be edified, discovered, developed and deployed. This is our divine duty, our great mission and our grace-filled New Testament role.

Prophets Equip the Saints

Another part of our mission from God as prophets and prophetesses is to join the fivefold ministry (apostles, prophets, evangelists, pastors and teachers) in equipping the saints with the tools necessary to extend the Kingdom into the farthest corners of the planet. Here is what Paul had to say about this role:

> But to each one of us grace was given according to the measure of Christ's gift. . . .
> And He gave some as apostles, and some as prophets, and some as evangelists, and some as pastors and teachers, for the equipping of the saints for the work of service, to the

building up of the body of Christ; until we all attain to the unity of the faith, and of the knowledge of the Son of God, to a mature man, to the measure of the stature which belongs to the fullness of Christ. As a result, we are no longer to be children, tossed here and there by waves and carried about by every wind of doctrine, by the trickery of men, by craftiness in deceitful scheming; but speaking the truth in love, we are to grow up in all aspects into Him who is the head, even Christ, from whom the whole body, being fitted and held together by what every joint supplies, according to the proper working of each individual part, causes the growth of the body for the building up of itself in love.

Ephesians 4:7, 11–16

We have briefly investigated these verses already, but my purpose here is to help you discover all the different responsibilities of the prophet and prophetess. I will talk more about how prophets and prophetesses practically equip the saints, but here let's glean what we can from these verses about our prophetic responsibility. The first thing we see is that the prophet is part of the fivefold team of people who equip the saints. The outcome of this team's ministry to the saints is that the body builds itself up in love.

In my experience and as a general overview, pastors and teachers have been good at helping people learn how to help themselves. Pastors are good at teaching people how to have their needs met through God, and they also help those they are in relationship with get healthy. Teachers have generally done a fair job of giving people tools so that they can glean revelation from the Scriptures for themselves.

In my opinion, though, historically speaking I do not think apostles, evangelists and prophets have done nearly as good a job in their specific areas of grace at equipping people. For example, evangelists are commonly thought of as people who do crusades or in some manner lead others to Christ. They are not often thought of as ministers who equip the Body of Christ to reach the lost. In other words, evangelists produce, but they seldom reproduce themselves through other people.

The same could be said of prophets. We tend to be the people others go to for prophetic insight, but we certainly have not become famous for reproducing our prophetic gift in other people. Of course, I am not saying that prophets should reproduce other prophets. God calls certain people as prophets; we do not call them. Yet prophets can and should help younger, less experienced prophets grow and learn.

My main point here is that prophets have a responsibility to help impart and grow the *gift of prophecy* in the lives of the saints. I want to talk more about that in a minute, but first I want to point out that we prophets are part of the fivefold team that helps people grow up and become solid in doctrine. We teach people how to use discernment in their interaction with others so that they are not tricked, schemed against and preyed upon. Prophets and prophetesses also teach people how to speak the truth in love (not to love to speak the truth or enjoy rebuking people). The outcome of all this is that the people of God get along as they go along. They figure out where they fit in the Body, and they learn that their lives were divinely designed to meet needs in a community of believers that no one else could ever fulfill.

Let's also contrast some of the passage from Ephesians 4 that we just read with a passage from Romans 12, which will give you an overview of how the saints are equipped through the fivefold ministry. Here is the portion from Romans I want to look at:

> Since we have gifts that differ according to the grace given to us, each of us is to exercise them accordingly: if prophecy,

according to the proportion of his faith; if service, in his serving; or he who teaches, in his teaching; or he who exhorts, in his exhortation; he who gives, with liberality; he who leads, with diligence; he who shows mercy, with cheerfulness.

Romans 12:6–8

When we contrast these two portions of Scripture, a beautiful picture of grace begins to emerge from the pages of these letters. Notice first that Paul says to the Ephesians that grace was given to us according to Christ's gift. We have already discovered that "Christ's gifts" are specifically the fivefold ministers. This means that the apostle, prophet, evangelist, pastor and teacher equip the saints with grace. In the book of Romans, we learn that we all have gifts that differ according to the grace given to us, and that we are to exercise these gifts according to the proportion of our faith. Putting it all together, we see that the fivefold ministers each equip us with grace, and it is this grace that equips us with different gifts.

I like to explain it like this: Let's pretend for a minute that the fivefold ministry is like a soda fountain, and that each minister is a flavor. For the sake of visualizing my metaphor, just imagine that we have Coke, 7-UP, Dr Pepper, root beer and grape soda. They all five have soda water in common, but the individual fountains determine the flavor. If you want grape soda, you cannot go to the Coke dispenser; you must go to the grape soda dispenser. And the amount of soda you dispense is determined by the size of the container you bring to the fountain.

In my metaphor, the five flavors of soda are the different fivefold ministers, and the flavors themselves are the different kinds of grace that flow from each of the fivefold offices. If you need prophetic grace that equips you with prophetic gifts, you cannot go to the pastoral fountain; you must instead fill your container at the prophet's fountain. But the amount of grace that you receive from each of the fivefold fountains is determined by the proportion of faith (metaphorically speaking, the size of the container) that you bring to the fountain.

It is necessary to understand that grace is not just undeserved favor; it is the operational power of God. It is the ability to do what you could not do one second before you received His grace. Furthermore, grace is multidimensional in its enabling power, so that different gifts are birthed from different types of grace. Jesus said with reference to prophets that if you receive a prophet in the name of a prophet, you will receive a prophet's reward. But He also went on to explain that if you receive a prophet in the name of a righteous man, you will only get a righteous man's reward (see Matthew 10:41). This indicates that the value you place on the office determines the power you receive from it.

When Jesus walked the earth, He was obviously the Body of Christ—the entire fivefold ministry embodied in one person. When Jesus said that He saw the people as sheep without a shepherd, He was demonstrating His pastoral grace. When He talked about the shepherd who left the ninety-nine to go after the one, He was demonstrating His evangelistic grace. When He responded to being called "Rabbi" by the people, He was demonstrating His fivefold teaching grace. When Jesus said that He had been sent from the Father to do the Father's will, He was demonstrating His apostolic grace. Finally, when Jesus shouted out he who has eyes to see, let him see, and he who has ears to hear, let him hear, He was demonstrating the grace that flows from the office of the prophet.

Prophets give people eyes to see and ears to hear. One of the most important functions prophets and prophetesses have in the Body of Christ is to equip each member of the Church to hear from God for himself or herself, and for others in need.

It is one sign of a highly dysfunctional spiritual community when the prophets or prophetesses become the main source of hearing from God. The primary responsibility of the office of the prophet and prophetess is to create a prophetic community where every member of the Body understands how to give and receive prophetic words.

At Bethel Church, after each service we make available a team of people who are trained to minister to the congregation. They are equipped to heal the sick, cast out demons and prophesy to people in need. Often I will come to the front to join the ministry team, but in doing so, I have learned that people will line up in front of me to get a word from the Lord instead of receiving ministry from the rest of the team. It would be unhealthy for me to allow or encourage that. As much as I love ministering to people, I refuse to be a mediator between them and God. I know there is a delicate balance I need to keep because as prophets and prophetesses, we do need to demonstrate what we articulate. I need to be up there ministering to others prophetically, but I do not desire to be the "main attraction" in any way. The Body of Christ desperately needs multiple role models whom they can follow so they can understand how to walk in the prophetic impartation they have received.

A Little History Lesson

In the early 1980s and '90s, God again began to restore the office of the prophet to the Body of Christ. It was exciting to watch prophets like Paul Cain and Bob Jones demonstrate their powerful prophetic ministry from the podium. But the ramification of that season was that people often came to "watch the show" or to get a prophetic word.

These prophets, through no fault of their own, became like superstars. They operated at such a high level of prophetic revelation that not only were people unequipped themselves, but they also often felt disqualified.

I love these men and others like them. Bob Jones was like a father to me. He literally saved my life when I went through the "dark night of the soul." I recently mourned his passing. But I am thankful that this season in the Body of Christ has dramatically changed, so that the emphasis has shifted from the formidable superstars to a powerful royal priesthood who can literally demonstrate the raw power of God everywhere they go.

Prophets and prophetesses do not need large sanctuaries filled with people in which to minister. Instead, they are seeping into every crack and crevice of society and demonstrating to a dark world the light and power of a superior Kingdom. It is levied upon us as prophets and prophetesses to prepare the sons and daughters of the King to push back the darkness and to build with light everywhere they go.

Prophets Commission Leaders

One of the most exciting elements of the call of God on the lives of prophets and prophetesses is that we often get the privilege of commissioning people into their divine destiny. The prophet Samuel anointed both Saul and David as kings. Here is one of those accounts: "Then Samuel took the flask of oil, poured it on his [Saul's] head, kissed him and said, 'Has not the LORD anointed you a ruler over His inheritance?' (1 Samuel 10:1). Here is the other: "And the LORD said, 'Arise, anoint him; for this is he.' Then Samuel took the horn of oil and anointed him in the midst of his brothers; and the

Spirit of the Lord came mightily upon David from that day forward" (1 Samuel 16:12–13).

My favorite commissioning story in the entire Bible is when the prophet Moses commissioned Joshua in the wilderness. The story gives us some incredible insights into what actually takes place when the prophets of God commission a person. God has just told Moses that he cannot go into the Promised Land, and in fact, that He is taking Moses home. Moses beseeches the Lord to not leave his congregation without a shepherd. (It is easy to see why God chose Moses as the leader of His people. Over and over again, Moses demonstrated great love for the people whom God had called him to lead.) Take a closer look at the story:

> So the Lord said to Moses, "Take Joshua the son of Nun, a man in whom is the Spirit, and lay your hand on him; and have him stand before Eleazar the priest and before all the congregation, and *commission* him in their sight. You shall put some of your *authority* on him, in order that all the congregation of the sons of Israel may obey him. Moreover, he shall stand before Eleazar the priest, who shall inquire for him by the judgment of the Urim before the Lord. At his command they shall go out and at his command they shall come in, both he and the sons of Israel with him, even all the congregation." Moses did just as the Lord commanded him; and he took Joshua and set him before Eleazar the priest and before all the congregation. Then he laid his hands on him and *commissioned* him, just as the Lord had spoken through Moses.
>
> Numbers 27:18–23, emphasis added

The most powerful insight I see in this story is that God told Moses to commission Joshua by giving him some of his authority. The Hebrew word here for authority is *hod*, which means "splendor, majesty, vigor, authority, beauty, glory and honor." In other words, when the prophet Moses commissioned Joshua, it was not just a ceremony in the sight of the people to pass the baton. No! Instead, Moses was literally passing his mantle of majesty, splendor, glory, vigor and honor to his successor.

This mantle affected Joshua's leadership in two important ways. First, it gave Joshua leadership abilities that he did not have before he received Moses' authority. But second and just as importantly, the majestic effects of this mantle attracted the people to Joshua so that they were inspired to follow him. This is an example of that often indefinable dynamic that causes people to want to lay down their lives to follow someone. I have observed this kind of favor on only a few people in my entire lifetime. Bill Johnson is one of those leaders. He has this invisible but tangible kind of glory, majesty and splendor about him that causes people to want to leave everything to follow him.

Another interesting side note is that Eleazar the priest was commanded to bring only the Urim to the commissioning, and not the Thummim. The Levitical priests carried the Urim and Thummim on their breastplate. Most theologians believe that the Urim and Thummim were two stones. The Thummim was a black stone representing the *No* of God, and the Urim was a white stone representing God's *Yes* and *Amen*. The interesting fact is that Moses told Eleazar to bring only the Urim—the *Yes* of God—because the decision concerning Joshua becoming Moses' successor had already been made by God and established by His prophet.

This is a great example of how the prophetic ministry functions at times. As prophets and prophetesses, we are called to have a team mentality and to work with the other fivefold ministers honorably and humbly. Our prophetic words should always be open to judgment and scrutiny by the leaders over us, by the other prophets who walk with us and by the people who are affected by our prophetic declarations. But there are times (on rare occasions) when God requires the rest of His royal priesthood simply to bring their *Yes* to the commissioning (or to a specific situation) that has already been prophetically established.

Mantles for Missions

When God commissions His leaders such as Joshua, He releases *mantles* over them. These mantles give them the supernatural ability to complete their mission. Unlike the gifts and call of God that remain on a person for life, a mantle stays with the *mission*, not with the person. For example, anyone who becomes president of the United States has to be a very gifted person. You do not rise to highest office in our land without amazing qualifications. But on the day of the inauguration, something powerful takes place in the spirit realm. A presidential mantle from heaven is given to the person who has been elected to that office.

God never grants someone an assignment without giving him or her the ability to complete it. God Himself establishes all authority in the universe; therefore every leadership role on the planet is a mission from God (see Romans 13:1). The presidential mantle gives these leaders the capacity to direct our country beyond their human ability. When their presidential term is over and they leave the White House, however, *the mantle stays with the mission* so it can be passed on to the next president. But those outgoing people's leadership gifts and calling remain with them.

Before Joshua ever received his mantle, he had the chance to experience the effects of the mantle that rested on the shoulders of Moses. One of the most striking examples of this is found in Exodus 17:8–13, the story of Joshua being commissioned by Moses to take his soldiers and go down in the valley to fight Amalek. During the battle, Moses went up on the mountain and held up his hands. When Moses got tired and dropped his arms, Joshua began to lose the battle. When Moses lifted up his arms, Joshua won. It became clear to the Israelite leadership that Joshua's victory was directly related to Moses raising his hands, so they put a leader on each side of Moses to help support his arms until Joshua won the battle and defeated Amalek.

New Testament Commissioning

We see this same principle of commissioning operating in the New Testament when the apostle Paul exhorted Timothy to be diligent with the gifts he had received through the laying on of hands by the prophetic presbytery. Here is a short excerpt from Paul's letter to Timothy:

> Do not neglect the spiritual gift within you, which was bestowed on you through prophetic utterance with the laying on of hands by the presbytery. Take pains with these things; be absorbed in them, so that your progress will be evident to all.
>
> 1 Timothy 4:14–15

The presbytery mentioned in this passage typically was made up of elders of the church who were not necessarily all prophets or prophetesses. But they had authority from God to commission leaders, and they moved powerfully in the prophetic ministry. Of course, this does not specifically establish the fact that prophets were the only ones commissioning people in the New Testament. It does, however, reaffirm that the prophetic ministry continued to play an important part in establishing leaders and their roles. In the case of Timothy, he was commissioned as an apostle to the church of Ephesus by the presbytery, which probably included the apostle Paul.

Let me make one final point about the impartation that takes place during the commissioning process. The apostle Paul wrote this to the church of Rome: "For I long to see you so that I may impart some spiritual gift to you, that you may be established" (Romans 1:11). The impartation that takes place through the prophets and apostles cannot be underestimated. Paul makes it clear to the Romans that the gift he is talking about cannot be established without his impartation. The Greek word for *established* is *sterizo*, which means "to confirm, to establish, to stand resolutely and to strengthen," and Paul makes it clear that he has to be present to do that. Since the scope of this book primarily concerns prophets and prophetesses, we are not investigating the office of the apostle in depth, but suffice to say that the apostles in the New Testament often played a significant role in commissioning leaders in the early Church. I cover the various aspects of the apostolic ministry in my book *How Heaven Invades Earth: Transform the World around You* (Regal, 2013).

I have had the privilege of commissioning many leaders into their divine call in almost every walk of life. I have often been part of presbyteries where we have commissioned leaders to one of the fivefold offices. I also have prophesied and commissioned many political leaders from several different countries into their God-given office, often long before they were actually elected.

Let me leave you with a final thought on the subject of commissioning leaders. I often wonder how the absence of the prophetic office has affected the leadership around the world. In other words, if Paul can say that the Romans are not established because of his absence, then I wonder how many countries, states and cities have leaders in place who carry no mantle or anointing for the office they inhabit, because of the lack of prophetic commissioning. And I wonder, just as importantly, how many offices have the wrong leaders in place. I do not have the answer to these questions, but it does create an urgency in me to see God's prophets and prophetesses take their proper places in the earth so that we can make disciples of all nations.

God's Secret Service

Let's take a look at a couple more exciting dynamics in the life of the prophet and prophetess. An Old Testament prophet named Amos opened up a real can of worms when he said, "Surely the Lord GOD does nothing unless He reveals His secret counsel to His servants the prophets" (Amos 3:7). Throughout history, God has always had a special relationship with His prophets. Bob Jones used to tell me, "Men are famous on earth for the things they share, but prophets are famous in heaven for the secrets they keep."

As prophets and prophetesses, it is important for us to realize that God tells us His secrets—things He does not want anyone else to know. I often wonder if the level of anointing in our lives is directly related to our ability not to brag about the things God shares with us. Most of us probably do not even realize that God would tell us something that He would not tell anyone else, but that is the nature of God's relationship with His prophets. Prophets and prophetesses are God's Secret Service!

This leads me to another point: Because God tells His prophets His secrets, it stands to reason that we should ask

His permission to share the things He reveals to us. Sometimes God shares things He wants us to deal with only in prayer. I wonder if God feels betrayed when He tells us His secrets and we tell the world about them? I am sure it is often done innocently because we have not recognized the nature of our relationship with God. But we are all responsible for the revelation we have, and now that you are aware of this dynamic, you are responsible to keep God's secrets.

God Protects His Prophets

God has also been known to protect His prophets even when they are wrong. I certainly do not mean to condone a prophet's bad behavior by stating this. I am simply pointing out that God has favored His prophets for generations. This story about Abraham and Sarah is a great example of the way God has protected His prophets:

> Now Abraham journeyed from there toward the land of the Negev, and settled between Kadesh and Shur; then he sojourned in Gerar. Abraham said of Sarah his wife, "She is my sister." So Abimelech king of Gerar sent and took Sarah. But God came to Abimelech in a dream of the night, and said to him, "Behold, you are a dead man because of the woman whom you have taken, for she is married." Now Abimelech had not come near her; and he said, "Lord, will You slay a nation, even though blameless? Did he not himself say to me, 'She is my sister'? And she herself said, 'He is my brother.' In the integrity of my heart and the innocence of my hands I have done this." Then God said to him in the dream, "Yes, I know that in the integrity of your heart you have done this, and I also kept you from sinning against Me; therefore I did not let you touch her. Now therefore, restore

the man's wife, for he is a prophet, and he will pray for you and you will live."

Genesis 20:1–7

Although Abraham lied about Sarah being his sister, God still protected him. In fact, God told King Abimelech that if he touched Abraham's wife, He would kill him. God went on to say (in so many words), "You better restore Abraham's wife if you want to live, and you better have him pray for you, because he's a prophet."

I understand that this is an Old Testament example, and by giving it I am in no way trying to say that God kills people who mess with His prophets. Rather, I am pointing out that God tends to favor His prophets and prophetesses. As I mentioned earlier, some people believe that the greater the call is on their life, the more warfare there is against them. I have known prophets who wear sickness like a badge of honor, almost like a Purple Heart. Yet I am convinced that God protects the people He promotes, and that this is especially true with His servants the prophets.

I have experienced God's divine protection many times throughout my life. Long before I knew God, He was already protecting me. I attended an extremely violent high school and graduated in 1973. Our school was almost equally divided into three ethnic groups: African Americans, Latinos and Caucasians. This was during the Black Power days, so our campus was a war zone. As a white freshman (though I am actually Spanish), I walked the halls of our school feeling terrified of being mugged. One day while class was in session, I was walking down an empty area by myself on my way to the restroom. It was a covered sidewalk that followed the outline of the building, and suddenly this big, white guy stepped out from around a corner and grabbed me. He picked me up by

152

my shirt and began to shake me like a rag doll, while shouting obscenities at me.

"Da, da, dude, wh . . . wh . . . what is your pro . . . pro . . . problem?" I stuttered.

"I heard what you said about me, you little jerk!" he shouted (using a different word for me).

"Wo . . . wow, ma . . . man, I don't even know who ya are," I stammered, while all the strength drained from my body in fear.

He slung me to the ground and jumped on top of me. Then he started wailing on my face with his fist while continuing to scream accusations in my ear. Scared stiff, I was lying there with my eyes closed, helpless and afraid to move.

Then suddenly, I heard a deep voice say, "Get off my friend now!"

I opened my eyes just in time to see a huge man who looked like a bodybuilder grab the guy and lift him up by his neck, slamming him against the wall over and over.

Each time he banged him against the wall, he said repeatedly, "Kris is my friend! Do you understand me? Nobody messes with my friends! Do you get me?"

The bully just kept eeking out, "Yeah! Okay, man, I hear you, dude!"

I stood up slowly, surveying my body for damage. Just then, the big guy let go of my attacker. The bully's weakened body slid down the wall and landed curled up in a ball on the concrete sidewalk.

My mind swirled. *I've never seen either one of these guys before*, I thought. *What's going on here?*

My rescuer stared into my eyes and said, "If this guy gives you any more problems, let me know!"

"Okay," I said, my body still shaking like a leaf.

He walked down the hall about thirty yards and suddenly disappeared right before my eyes. Was he an angel? I guess

153

so. All I know is that I have had many experiences like this over the years, where God chose to protect me supernaturally. Actually, I kind of like it.

Prophets Protect Nations

God has called His prophets and prophetesses to protect nations. But before I go on, I must tell you that I actually contemplated leaving this final prophetic role out of this book because of its potentially destructive connotations. For one thing, saying that prophets protect nations has an Old Testament judgment sort of feel that is impossible for me to embrace on this side of the cross. Furthermore, it creates an "us and them," "good guy, bad guy" mentality. Of course, this was very much the mindset of the Old Testament Jewish people. They were the good guys and the Gentile nations were the bad guys, and God protected the "good people" from the "evil people." But as we discussed already, God has commanded us in the New Testament dispensation to love our enemies and be kind to those who hate us.

Yet I do need to include this prophetic role here because as I travel the world, I remain convinced that there are nations, as well as people groups, that are bent on the destruction of others. God has literally woken me up in the middle of the night many times to prophesy against violent acts of terror— too many times for me to ignore this vital role of the prophet and prophetess.

As I said, this principle of prophets protecting nations is easy to demonstrate in the Old Testament. For example, the prophet Isaiah made this prophetic declaration when the Assyrian king was out to destroy Judah in the days of Hezekiah:

Thus you shall say to your master, "Thus says the LORD, 'Do not be afraid because of the words that you have heard, with which the servants of the king of Assyria have blasphemed Me. Behold, I will put a spirit in him so that he will hear a rumor and return to his own land. And I will make him fall by the sword in his own land.'"

2 Kings 19:6–7

The prophet Elisha also protected the king of Israel when the king of Aram was out to destroy the Israelites. Aram developed secret battle plans and shared them only with his most trusted commanders. But what he did not realize was that Israel had a superhero, a prophet named Elisha who had supernatural powers. His superhero gifts gave him the ability to perceive the top-secret plans of the enemy and reveal them to the king of Israel.

Naturally, King Aram thought he had a traitor among his commanders when he discovered that the king of Israel was always prepared to thwart his devious plans. Finally growing angry, King Aram interrogated his commanders, looking for the traitor who was conspiring against him:

Now the heart of the king of Aram was enraged over this thing; and he called his servants and said to them, "Will you tell me which of us is for the king of Israel?" One of his servants said, "No, my lord, O king; but Elisha, the prophet who is in Israel, tells the king of Israel the words that you speak in your bedroom."

2 Kings 6:11–12

The enemy king decided to try to arrest the prophet Elisha, which did not work out very well for the king at all. I will let you read the rest of that story for yourself in the sixth chapter of 2 Kings, but undoubtedly, God's prophets were instrumental in the protection of His people.

This Side of the Cross

On this side of the cross, though, the million-dollar question is this: How do we love our enemies, live to reconcile people to God by not counting their trespasses against them and keep the core values of the Kingdom while simultaneously using our supernatural gifts to protect our nations? I am not sure there is a simple solution to this complicated problem, but I will attempt to answer the question using the prophecy I gave on February 19, 2012.

Before I share that prophecy with you, let me set the scene. Four major issues were occurring at that time. First, President Obama was running for his second term, and conservative Republicans were hoping that Mitt Romney would win the election. Personally I was voting for Romney, but the Lord spoke to me in January of that year and told me He was "giving President Obama another chance." From that word, I knew our president would win a second term. The second issue pressing on the hearts of Americans was that our economy was in a recession, which many thought would soon lead to a depression. The third and fourth issues were that Iran was threatening Israel with nuclear war, while North Korea was building a war machine and threatening America and its allies.

In the midst of that economic and political turmoil, this is the prophecy that I gave publicly to our congregation on that Sunday morning in February:

> I have a sense that our country is improving. I had a vision of God blowing or breathing on this continent as Jesus breathed on His disciples and said, "Receive the Holy Spirit." It wasn't a suggestion, but a command. I saw the nation turning blood red from the East Coast to the West Coast. It was the redemptive nature of forgiveness being assimilated into the ground . . . and out of the soil, souls were emerging like

156

soldiers in a battlefield. Dead bones were coming to life. They were dressed for battle in different realms. Some had expensive business suits and others were dressed like doctors, teachers, mothers and so forth. They all were given secret messages that they read and then ate. The messages transformed them and equipped them for their mission. Revelation was released over the nation, and inventions and innovations were springing up all over like flowers during the first week of spring. Pennsylvania was highlighted as if a major breakthrough was rising from there. Instead of two towers, three towers were being built as a sign of the strength of the economy being supported by a three-cord strand. I felt a warning that many would look at the political climate to determine the condition of the country, but the signs of revival would not flow *from* the White House, but *to* it. Hope would not arise from the polls, but from the people. This was a people movement that swept the globe, turning the planet a deep purple.

I saw the Lord blowing freezing cold air over Iran and North Korea. It created impossible conditions for war. He literally froze their war machines. . . . It was a political climate change equal to the fall of the Iron Curtain.

Every country that was bent on war was frozen. . . . The climate was suddenly and unpredictably changed. It was strange, but good.

I saw that God had already released Daniels into China, and humility and generosity would spring up from the East. God called it a "helps movement." I saw that China would be given the "gift of helps" for the world. God was hugging centuries of brokenness out of China. I heard the words *singing revolution*.

I really feel as though that prophesy signified that in my country, America, we are in a good season. But just to be clear, I do not think the political climate of my country will determine what God is doing. I do not think the Lord is leading with politicians right now. I do not mean that He never does.

In fact, I do think there are countries outside America where the main move of God is coming from the political realm. But I do not think that in the next several years, that will be demonstrated here in the United States. I do not think you can look to a person for the answer. One single person is not going to usher in this dramatic change that I see happening in our country. I think it is a people movement. I think the Lord is doing it all among the people, and I think many people will rise up and become powerful. They will also become famous, if you will, in this movement. But they probably will not be the people whom we vote for in our elections.

At the time of that prophetic word, the Lord said, "Don't look to the political climate to determine what I'm doing in America in the next four years." In other words, He was saying not to get excited or disappointed by what is happening in the political climate, because He has chosen a different venue for this season. I also had a vision of three towers. I saw the Lord rise up, and I saw generosity and humility come to our nation. I saw that generosity, humility and stewardship are going to begin to break the back of poverty and debt. Invention and innovation are going to begin to flow out of America again.

The Outcome

Of course, by now some of my 2012 prophecy has already come to pass. President Obama was reelected to a second term, and the political climate did not change. Yet the American economy has continued to improve slowly instead of winding down into a depression, as many economists predicted. And on February 29, 2012, literally just ten days after my public prophecy, Fox News ran an article online entitled "US: North

Korea suspends nuclear activities, takes food aid." Here is an interesting quote from that article (emphasis added):

> After an *especially difficult winter in 2011*, the U.N. World Food Program launched an emergency operation to make up for a decline in humanitarian assistance and the country's own decision to buy only limited purchases of food staples.
>
> Before the elder Kim's death, the two sides had appeared close to reaching agreement on the U.S. providing "nutritional assistance" to needy women, children and the elderly, and North Korea freezing its uranium enrichment. Such a *freeze* was meant to lead to six-nation aid-for-disarmament talks that North Korea withdrew from in 2009.[1]

This was just one of two articles written about North Korea "*freezing* its nuclear plan" right after I gave this prophetic word. The other article also appeared exactly ten days after my prophecy on Yahoo! News online and was entitled "U.S. announces diplomatic breakthrough with North Korea."[2]

As I write this book, the urgency in Iran has passed for now, and North Korea continues to be held in check. The more pressing global issues revolve around Russia and the Ukraine. I am not naïve enough to believe that there will ever be a time when there is not trouble in the nations or between nations. But my deep prophetic sense is that we are entering a new epoch season where war, in the overall general sense, will become an obsolete way to solve issues between countries.

In fact, I have been praying heavily into the following passage out of Isaiah 2. I will leave you to contemplate the possible

1. "US: North Korea suspends nuclear activities, takes food aid," *Associated Press*, February 29, 2012, http://www.foxnews.com/politics/2012/02/29/us-north -korea-suspends-nuclear-activities/.
2. Laura Rozen, "U.S. announces diplomatic breakthrough with North Korea," February 29, 2012, http://news.yahoo.com/blogs/envoy/u-announces-diplomatic -breakthrough-north-korea-152331635.html.

supernatural ramifications of Isaiah's 2,500-year-old procla-
mation as you read it for yourself:

The word which Isaiah the son of Amoz saw concerning
Judah and Jerusalem.

Now it will come about that
In the last days
The mountain of the house of the LORD
Will be established as the chief of the mountains,
And will be raised above the hills;
And all the nations will stream to it.
And many peoples will come and say,
"Come, let us go up to the mountain of the LORD,
To the house of the God of Jacob;
That He may teach us concerning His ways
And that we may walk in His paths."
For the law will go forth from Zion
And the word of the LORD from Jerusalem.
And He will judge between the nations,
And will render decisions for many peoples;
And they will hammer their swords into plowshares
    and their spears into pruning hooks.
Nation will not lift up sword against nation,
And never again will they learn war.

Isaiah 2:1–4

As I read through this passage and pray into it, my honest
question is this: Why not here, and why not now?

7

BUILDING A
PROPHETIC COMMUNITY

Prophets and prophetesses have a responsibility to develop a prophetic culture both locally and globally. Before we press into the details of this important subject, though, I want you to know that I am making a few assumptions about you if you are someone who is going to read and apply this chapter. First of all, I am assuming that you are part of a local church that has empowered you to shepherd the prophetic people. (You can refer back to chapter 1, where I recount my own story, to refresh your understanding about what I mean by "empowering you.") Second, I am assuming that you have read through and embraced chapter 4 on core values, and that you have worked Kingdom core values into your life. This is crucial because poor or distorted core values will quickly pollute not only your prophetic ministry, but also the prophetic culture you are helping develop. And third, I am assuming that you include, as much as possible, the rest of the fivefold ministry in the equipping and training process of your prophetic community. This is essential in establishing a healthy prophetic company.

I also want you to understand that I will not address the subject of the gift of prophecy much more in this book. I already mentioned that I have written some other books (and articles) on the subject. The emphasis of this chapter will be on developing a prophetic culture and community. If you need materials that will help you develop the gift of prophecy in the lives of your prophetic people, I suggest that you make use of some of my other materials.[1]

Developing a Prophetic Culture

There is a major difference between prophetic ministry and a healthy prophetic culture. Ministry is simply the ability to perform in a way that hopefully helps people. On the other hand, when cultures emerge they exert a dynamic influence on people's mindsets, which affects the way they live, love and behave.

A culture is like an invisible yet powerful river, a concept that cannot always be explained. But everyone who is in the community sharing that culture undeniably experiences it. Like the current of a river, a culture naturally flows toward a common destination. You can resist it or swim against the stream, but the outcome will be exhaustion.

1. For this purpose, I again suggest that you make use of my book *Basic Training for the Prophetic Ministry*. A curriculum kit is available that goes along with the book and includes video segments in which I guide you through the lessons and the principles they cover. The curriculum can be studied in groups or individually.

Culture in itself is not necessarily positive or negative. Every community has a culture that is developed either in-actively, reactively or proactively. Healthy cultures require proactive leaders who define the divine destiny of their people and then develop the banks of the river to direct its current to a predetermined outcome.

In the following pages, I want to describe to you the "banks" of a prophetic river that are necessary to build a healthy prophetic community. Most of what I share with you comes from my own experience—especially that of doing it wrong, getting it wrong and teaching it wrong. For me, this led to many sleepless nights of wrestling with God for answers that would help our prophetic community become whole. My heart is that you would learn from my limp and not have the same painful experiences I had, only to discover the identical revelation I got.

Risk

Risk is the first of a series of elements that must be cultivated among your people to develop a healthy prophetic culture. I propose to you that risk is actually a part of the very nature of God. Look at the beginning of creation. God did not childproof the Garden. Instead, He planted two trees there, the Tree of Life and the Tree of the Knowledge of Good and Evil. The latter would kill a person within 24 hours of eating its fruit (see Genesis 2:17). God gave humankind the chance to live forever, but only at the risk of the death penalty.

Let's look at another great example of the risky life of the Kingdom. Jesus went to a wedding party with His twelve guys and His mother. After the wedding guests had partied for a long time, the host ran out of wine. Mary pressed her Son into making more wine. John records the incident in his gospel:

> When the headwaiter tasted the water which had become wine, and did not know where it came from (but the servants who had drawn the water knew), the headwaiter called the bridegroom, and said to him, "Every man serves the good wine first, and when the people have drunk freely, then he serves the poorer wine; but you have kept the good wine until now."
>
> John 2:9–10

The words "drunk freely" in this passage are translated from the Greek word *methuo*. It means "to be drunk or intoxicated." Jesus made wine for people who were already drunk! Was God condoning drunkenness? Of course not. There is no way that the Lord wanted people to get drunk. The Bible makes that clear in several other passages (see Galatians 5:19–21; Ephesians 5:18). But Jesus left it up to those present to decide how much they would have to drink.

At this point you might be asking yourself, *Why does Jesus want to give people such choices?* The answer is simple: God has developed a Kingdom of reward. The only way to be rewarded for doing the right thing is to have the ability to choose to do the wrong thing. The writer of the book of Hebrews put it this way: "Without faith it is impossible to please Him, for he who comes to God must believe that He is and that He is a rewarder of those who seek Him" (Hebrews 11:6).

God does not control people. He actually provides them with options and then empowers them to make great choices. It is the nature of religion to create cultural sanitization by eliminating people's choices. Metaphorically speaking, we cut down the second tree in the Garden or remove the wine from the wedding, then we redefine this kind of action as sanctification. But it is not sanctification; it is control.

The challenge for us as prophets and prophetesses is that we must train and equip our prophetic people with their deployment in mind. But it is nearly impossible to train in the zoo and still have our people ready for the reality of the jungle, so to speak. This is the main reason why prophecy has been reduced to staying within the four walls of the church, while the psychics direct the nations. This kind of insanity must stop!

One way to put a stop to it is for us as prophets and prophetesses to train our people in an environment that prepares them to impact the world. This means we have to develop prophetic exercises with a high level of risk so that our prophetic people know what it feels like to get it wrong. They can then learn to develop a proactive plan to reduce the fallout, while cleaning up their mess.

Let me give you a practical example of how to foster a culture of risk in your environment. We have about a thousand new students come to the Bethel School of Supernatural Ministry every year from all over the world. The students are understandably nervous the first week of school, which creates a perfect environment in which they can face their fears. They are usually wondering if they have what it takes to be part of a "supernatural school." By the second day, I have them all stand up and form groups of two with someone they do not know.

Then I give them this instruction: "Grab hands with the person you are with and ask the Holy Spirit the name of the person's mother or where she was born."

I go on to say, "You will have thirty seconds, which is plenty of time to hear from the Holy Spirit, so don't be nervous. Now pray quietly until I tell you to give the other person the word of knowledge you receive."

I also add, "Oh, by the way, we just have one rule regarding this exercise. You can't say that you didn't get anything from the Holy Spirit. If you don't get something, then just guess!"

The students all laugh nervously as they pray.

Finally I shout, "Okay, tell the person you're with what you got from the Holy Spirit. And one more thing—turn off your mercy gift and tell each other whether or not you got it right."

By this time, the tension in the room is so thick that you can cut it with a knife. I intentionally make sure there is no music or worship going on during this exercise, and I also tease the students while they are trying to concentrate.

A few minutes later, when the students are done dialoging with each other, I say to everyone, "Whoever got the word of knowledge wrong, please raise your hand up high!"

It is always kind of funny watching everyone look around to see who will be the first to raise his or her hand. But within a minute or so, at my continued exhortation, they finally all raise their hands, perhaps with a few exceptions of those who got it right. Then I have them all clap and celebrate one another. They do not really know what to think about this exercise, but unbeknownst to them, they have begun to learn three powerful lessons:

1. You must face your fears to move in faith.
2. God does not punish you when you get it wrong, and neither do we.
3. The only way you get good at knowing the voice of the Holy Spirit is to practice and then get feedback.

Prophetic revelation grows in an R&D (research and development) culture. Let me explain what I mean by giving you an example from the business world. The product sales and manufacturing industry is divided into two main divisions that have competing core values. The manufacturing division of a company has a "zero defect" core value, while the research and development division has an "experiment and discover by trial and error" core value.

When Apple Corporation went to market with its new iPhone, for instance, the goal of the manufacturing department was to have no defects whatsoever in the phones they were selling. But the R&D department, which invented the iPhone, probably made hundreds of mistakes in the process of developing the product. If Apple tried to apply the same core values to its R&D department as it did to its manufacturing division, the company would never invent any products. In other words, even though both divisions are part of the same great company, success in these two departments is measured much differently. Mistakes are inevitable in the invention process, but they are the demise of production.

To apply this to the prophetic, it is impossible to create a healthy prophetic culture while embracing a "zero defects" core value in ministry. In shaping the banks of the prophetic river we are part of, we must celebrate the experimental research and discovery process that empowers revelation. That is not to say that there is no place for "zero defects." Our individual character and our relationship with God are the areas in which we should strive for zero defects. These are the things that belong in the "manufacturing department," so to speak. But the R&D departments of the Church include learning to apply truth, experimenting with the Holy Spirit, moving in the gifts, stepping out in faith, dreaming with God, attempting the impossible, believing the unreasonable and so on. Metaphorically speaking, both departments exist in the same people.

In reality, we must learn to balance the priorities of risk taking and excellence in all areas of life—in our character development, in our relationships and in our pursuit of prophetic revelation. The problem is that risk taking creates messes, exposes flaws and, more often than not, teaches us what *does not work*. But this is the process that leads to true spiritual maturity.

As prophets and prophetesses who are equipping the saints, we must proactively develop cultures that equip people to face the reality of who they are and empower them to take responsibility for their messes. And we must accomplish all this without controlling them. As passionately as we long to see everyone walking in wholeness, we have to remind ourselves that you cannot punish people into purity, because holiness is an inside job.

Many years ago, one of our students came to us from another very large ministry school (which, by the way, is gone now). He told me a sad story about his former school. One afternoon, a senior staff member asked all the students who were struggling with pornography to stand up so that they could pray for them. Nearly three hundred students stood up in the class of a thousand. They prayed fervently and passionately for these students, but the next day they expelled every one of them.

I understand that we are talking about character here and not prophetic ministry. I agree that character matters and that the blood of Jesus is so powerful that pornography should have no hold on our lives. And I also know that there are times when people refuse to repent and therefore "behave their way out of ministry." (Although we certainly still love them and accept them as people valuable to their Creator, whatever condition they are in.) Yet my point is that expelling all the students who stood up for prayer created a culture of punishment in that school and taught the students three things:

1. Do not be honest with people because they will punish you for it.

Building a Prophetic Community

2. Do not trust your leadership because they are out to get you.

3. I must be a bad person, unworthy of love from the leaders I respect the most.

The truth is, many spiritual leaders are afraid of sin. They have spent too much time in the zoo and too little time in the jungle, so they create cultures that refuse to tolerate sin because they feel powerless to help people process their way into purity.

Coaches and Referees

I love to play basketball, but the problem is that I have never played on an official team. It is not as if I never tried; I was just never good enough to actually make a team. Now I play pickup games at the YMCA about three times a week. There is a stark difference between the way I play and the way the guys who have actually been part of an official team play (which is most of the other guys). The challenge is that I have never had a basketball coach who taught me how to play the game the right way. Neither have I ever played in a game where a referee is calling fouls.

Consequently, most of the guys who actually know how to play basketball are not really fond of having me on the court with them. In pickup basketball, there is virtually no penalty for fouling someone, not to mention the fact that you never foul out of a game. And just as importantly, I never learned the proper shooting form, the right way to play defense or how to play strategically. For me, basketball has always been pretty much a free-for-all, kind of a no-blood/no-foul game. I frustrate the heck out of the guys who are really good. And

169

because these elements have been missing from my game from childhood, I have a hard time taking instruction from the guys on the court who know what they are doing. Hearing someone call a foul on me drives me crazy.

Prophets and prophetesses cannot be like that. They must create equipping cultures where there are coaches and referees. The coaches are expected to give feedback to the players, and the referees will call fouls when people behave in a way that is destructive to the game, so to speak. The Corinthians were basically making the prophetic ministry a free-for-all, so the apostle Paul taught them this:

> Let two or three prophets speak, and let the others pass judgment. But if a revelation is made to another who is seated, the first one must keep silent. For you can all prophesy one by one, so that all may learn and all may be exhorted; and the spirits of prophets are subject to prophets; for God is not a God of confusion but of peace. . . . All things must be done properly and in an orderly manner.
>
> 1 Corinthians 14:29–33, 40

In so many churches I visit, there is no prophetic culture because there are no coaches and no referees. It is just your basic prophetic pickup game. If prophets and prophetesses are going to transform dysfunctional prophetic ministries into healthy prophetic communities, we must create the expectation among our prophetic people that they are playing on a team. There is no place for selfish, independent and/or rebellious people who do not know how to honor leadership. The greatest challenge that many of us will experience is shifting the mindset of our prophetic people from being on the playground to being on global strike teams. Let me make three important observations from Paul's exhortation to the Corinthians:

1. Prophetic cultures require that every prophetic declaration is judged and scrutinized for its authentication and application.

2. The spirits of the prophets are subject to the prophets; therefore, everyone is personally responsible for their prophetic words. They cannot say, "The Holy Spirit came on me and I had no choice but to prophesy." The truth is that self-control is a fruit of the Holy Spirit.

3. God likes order (not to be confused with control), and although He may define it quite differently than we do, nevertheless, His spontaneity is always preplanned. After all, the Bible says that the "Lamb [was] slain from the foundation of the world" (Revelation 13:8 NKJV).

Empowering and Confronting

In the first chapter of this book, I mentioned how David's son Absalom clawed his way into the hearts of the people. The truth is that it takes a David to create an Absalom. David was a man after God's heart, and he knew how to kill giants. He was also an expert at equipping and empowering mighty men, who themselves became giant killers. Yet David had a major flaw in his leadership ability. He refused to confront his sons or his friends.

David's inability to confront the ones he loved the most caused him untold misery. Joab, the very capable commander-in-chief of David's entire army, murdered two other Israeli commanders out of jealousy. Still, King David refused to discipline him. Even more painful was the fact that three of David's undisciplined sons usurped his throne. Absalom even drove him out of his own country, yet David continually refused to confront any of them.

I want to make two points from this powerful illustration. First, if we want to raise up a prophetic company of people who are giant killers and can destroy the works of the devil, we must become empowering prophets and prophetesses who develop an empowering culture. As we talked about previously, leaders who are empowered allow people to experiment and to make mistakes. But such leaders also make decisions *with* people, not just *for* people. They do not withhold information or tell people only what they need to know to get the job done, because this produces slave camps in which one person does all the thinking. It is religion on steroids. Religion wants to tame people, domesticate the masses and get them to keep the rules. But prophetic revelation is never discovered behind the iron bars of the zoo.

Jesus is a great example of an empowering leader. He did not merely tell His disciples *what* to think; He taught them *how* to think. He did not keep them on the sidelines, watching Him do everything. They had permission to ask questions, to try to do what He was doing and to get feedback from Him. Jesus even exhorted His disciples to do even greater things than He did. True Kingdom-minded prophets and prophetesses are fathers and mothers who want their sons and daughters to succeed and exceed them.

The second lesson to learn from the life of David comes not from his successes, but from his failures. We must learn how to confront our people honorably at the same level that we empower them. Empowering people without confronting them promotes an ecosystem where Joabs and Absaloms germinate. Jesus had no problem confronting people. He did not oppose only the Pharisees and Sadducees; He often confronted His own disciples. He asked James and John what spirit they were of when they wanted to call down fire on the Samaritans. He called Peter "Satan" when he insisted on undermining the plan of Christ to die on the cross. He continually confronted all of His disciples' self-promoting and jealous attitudes with stories of humility and childlikeness. He made statements to them like, "How long must I be with you?" and "Why is your heart so hard?"

Healthy prophetic communities must have prophets and/or prophetesses who know how to skillfully confront the people whom they have empowered to minister. Like Jesus, they cannot be afraid to talk to their prophetic people about their attitudes, interactions and behaviors. Sometimes when I talk about confronting people, leaders picture some knock-down, drag-out fight. This is not at all what I have in mind when I am talking about developing a culture of confrontation. Confrontation should never be done in anger, nor should the goal be to punish people for their failures.

Let me give you a few keys I have learned over the years that will help us coach and referee the game of life in a way that creates wholesome prophetic communities. To start, let me say that you will never solve a conflict when

- The goal of the conversation is to prove you are right.

- You are determined that you know another person's motive.

- You are only listening to other people's words and not their hearts.

- You are angry and want to punish people, then you wonder why they do not want to tell you the truth. (If honesty is costly, then it will be hard for people to be totally forthright.)

- You bring up the past after you have said that you forgive someone. If people know you are keeping a file on their failures, they will not want to give you any more ammunition to use against them.

King Solomon put it like this: "Fools find no pleasure in understanding but delight in airing their own opinions" (Proverbs 18:2 NIV). We cannot let this be the commentary on our leadership. We have to ask God for an understanding heart as we labor to confront people, resolve conflict and bring wholeness to our prophetic community.

Solomon went on to say, "A gentle answer turns away wrath, but a harsh word stirs up anger" (Proverbs 15:1). Here are a few tools that will help resolve conflict:

1. De-escalate the offended person's anger by letting the person know that you believe in him or her and that you are there to listen. Keep the following dynamics in mind when you are dealing with someone who is angry to help bring closure to his or her situation:

   • Anger causes people to defend themselves instead of listen.

   • If you hold off confronting people until your anger overcomes your fear of confrontation, then your interaction will not come to a redemptive conclusion.

   • Warriors know how to deal with enemies, but they often do not know how to confront daughters and sons. They often wait until they are fed up with someone, then they rename their offender after an enemy such as Jezebel, Hitler or Judas. This is the first step toward cutting a person off from relationship instead of restoring him or her. We must take our armor off when we are working to solve a conflict or to bring closure to a hurting person.

2. Proverbs says, "The words of a gossip are like choice morsels; they go down to the inmost parts" (Proverbs 18:8 NIV). Refuse to be part of the secret witness program. The secret witness program is the dynamic that takes place when someone comes to you with an offense.

They tell you about "all the other people who agree" with them, but they refuse to give you anyone's name. Here is the principle of resolution in this situation: If you are not part of the problem and you are not part of the solution, then the issue is none of your business. Let me give you a few principles to remember to help dispel gossip from a prophetic community:

- Bitterness, jealousy and offense are magnetic forces that attract likeminded attitudes into their vortex. When people are offended with someone, everyone else who is offended with that person will mysteriously find them.

- Offense is like a virus that spreads through the air. It is caught through speech, body language and attitude.

- If someone has something against a person and speaks to you about it, your only response should be to send him or her back to the person with whom the problem originates. If you say nothing, your silence will be interpreted as agreeing with the offended person.

- When people come to talk to you, as soon as you have enough information to understand that they are offended, tell them you are a mandatory reporter in Jesus. It is your job to make sure that the person their conflict is with is informed, so before they continue talking, they might want to rethink their plan of spilling out all the evil they want to tell you about.

- I love the saying "unforgiveness is like drinking deadly poison and then thinking the other person is going to die." Forgiveness is the only 100 percent cure for bitterness and offense.

3. Solomon went on to say two more important things about counseling people: "The first to plead his case seems right, until another comes and examines him," and "Do you see a man wise in his own eyes? There is more hope for a fool than for him" (Proverbs 18:17;

26:12). When trying to bring closure to a situation, remember the following insights:

- Never come to a conclusion about who is right and who is wrong without hearing both sides of the story.

- You cannot help a person who does not have a problem. If a person who has an issue cannot see it, then nothing you or anyone else does will solve it.

- Help people understand how their behavior is affecting other people. Although we do not know people's motives, we do know how their attitude and behavior affect our culture. Mirror back the effects of their actions to them and let them decide what they are going to do about it.

- Get to the root of the problem. What is really wrong? Symptomatic cures do not solve root problems. Ask questions until you get to the heart of the real issue.

- People belong, believe and then behave, in that order. Do not settle for simply adjusting people's behavior. Determine how their connections and/or their core belief systems are playing into their dysfunctional behavior.

- Agree to an action plan that puts accountability in place. Issues that have become habits in people's lives are not magically fixed in one counseling session (at least not without a miracle). It is typically a proactive process that leads to total freedom in their lives. This usually requires some kind of discipleship, life coach and/or mentoring relationship—someone wise who can and will help walk people through the recovery process.

Testimonies

The final catalyst to a healthy prophetic culture I want to explore is the importance of *testimonies*. Testimonies help create an awareness of the works of God in our lives. This fosters an attitude of expectation, which creates an atmosphere where we are looking for what God has done and not what He has yet to do.

It is so easy for our prophetic people to fall into the trap of becoming hypersensitive to the negative activity in or around us. When we become problem focused, it robs us of our faith, steals our thankfulness and leads to high levels of anxiety. The often unspoken side effect of this mindset is that our prophetic people become very devil conscious. It does not take long before they end up with "a big devil, little God" mentality. This only serves to intensify their fears, which siphons off any anointing for ministry.

Fear is actually faith in the wrong god. Fear is the manifestation of *believing* that something is about to go wrong. And yet, "There is no fear in love; but perfect love casts out fear, because fear involves punishment, and the one who fears is not perfected in love" (1 John 4:18).

Testimonies are like a supernatural inoculation against fear's infection. The very act of reflecting on our day and proactively recalling God's activity opens up our hearts with gratitude toward Him. The psalmist put it like this: "Enter His gates with thanksgiving and His courts with praise" (Psalm 100:4).

Thanksgiving is our response to God's acts in our lives. Praise is our response to God's nature, to His attributes and to the reasons why He takes action in our lives. Thanksgiving is the key to accessing the Kingdom. Thanksgiving gestates in the garden of recollection and reflection on the acts of God. It is simply impossible to develop a healthy prophetic community without proactively embracing a culture of testimony.

The apostle John was exiled to the island of Patmos, where he penned the book of Revelation. In the midst of his trials,

John shared these powerful words: "The testimony of Jesus is the spirit of prophecy" (Revelation 19:10). In other words, what God did for someone else, He will do for us. When we forget the works of God, we lose sight of His ability to rescue us from any situation. The sons of Ephraim are a great example of what happens when we lose sight of God's supernatural activity in our lives. King David recalled what happened to them:

> The sons of Ephraim were archers equipped with bows, yet they turned back in the day of battle. They did not keep the covenant of God and refused to walk in His law; *they forgot His deeds and His miracles that He had shown them.*
>
> Psalm 78:9–11, emphasis added

David, a soldier himself, attributed the failure of these Ephriamite warriors in battle to forgetting the miracles that God had already accomplished in their lives. At Bethel Church, we work hard not to forget God's work in the lives of our people. In fact, we have a full-time staff member who oversees a whole team of people keeping track of the acts of God that take place among our congregation. It is our desire to steward testimonies the way some people steward property or finances. We proactively recount the works God has done so that we can remind ourselves of the miracles He is about to do. As the prophet Moses wrote, "You should diligently keep the commandments of the LORD your God, *and His testimonies*" (Deuteronomy 6:17, emphasis added).

We begin every meeting at Bethel with testimonies of God's miraculous intervention that we have witnessed in our circumstances. As I have stated already, this creates an atmosphere of expectation that the challenges we face every day will be met with God's ability, not our own. We often spend up to an hour sharing testimonies at our monthly board meeting, where finances are the most common item on the agenda. When we finally "get down to business," we approach Bethel's practical problems with faith in God's supernatural solutions already in mind.

Building a Faith Culture

How do we practically, purposefully build a culture of faith? I want to close this chapter by giving you a few practical tips on how you can shift the atmosphere in your prophetic community from fear to faith and from self-awareness to God-awareness, while simultaneously dismantling the "big devil, small God" complex.

Shifting the atmosphere into a faith culture involves attending to a few key things. If you will put into practice the following tips—stewarding the testimonies, identifying and shepherding what I call the "prophetic superheroes" and helping the fearful among you face their giants—it will go a long way toward establishing a healthy, faith-filled prophetic community. I want to look at each of these tips a little more closely with you.

Let testimonies foster faith

Shifting the atmosphere into a faith culture involves making sure that when your people meet, they share their testimonies. Testimonies foster a culture of faith and encourage hearts of gratitude. I just talked a few pages back about that and about what a high priority we put on stewarding our testimonies at Bethel Church, so I will not go into a lot of detail again here. But I recommend that you make testimonies a high priority, too, because stewarding the testimonies is a key step in practically, purposefully building a healthy prophetic culture.

On a corporate level, begin every meeting by having your people share stories of their prophetic exploits. Call to mind the things God has already done, which shifts the focus off what He has yet to do and puts it squarely on what He both can and will do as you follow Him.

It is important that you wisely guide these conversations, however, so that they remain healthy. As you direct these prophetic story exchanges, you will need to watch out for a few different scenarios and provide some guidance. Be ready to give some direction about who shares when, so that both beginners and what I call the "prophetic superheroes" can encourage others and be encouraged themselves.

Shepherd those with the superhero syndrome

Another key to building a healthy faith culture is keeping your eye on the "prophetic superheroes." There is almost always at least one "superhero" on our prophetic teams. These folks commonly have the most incredible stories of their prophetic exploits to tell. We want these people to share because it raises the bar in our prophetic community. They stretch us and remind the rest of the team that God wants to do greater things through them than they ever thought possible. But it is important to pastor these superhero people, because they tend to create an atmosphere in which people with "less spectacular" God stories do not want to share.

We also want beginners and people with less anointing to get in the habit of reflecting on the works of God in their lives and sharing them with the rest of our team, so I like to use some wisdom to think through how I allow our superhero/superstars to affect our prophetic community. With all this in mind, I often call on the quiet and/or less anointed people to share first. Specifically calling on these people says to them,

"I believe in you, and I'm expecting the Holy Spirit to move through you supernaturally."

I then celebrate their stories no matter how insignificant they seem. I also help them extract something from their testimony that perhaps they did not see at first. If the testimonies coming out of them are ridiculously unsupernatural, though, like "I got a new dog today" kind of stories, that is when I will call on my superstars to inspire greater levels of faith in the room through their testimonies.

I have pastored many "prophetic superheroes" in my ministry and have gained some insights into the things these people often (though not always) have in common. One thing to keep in mind is that sometimes these people simply exaggerate. I attribute this to the fact that most often, they need a lot of affirmation and attention. It feels extremely validating to them to share their stories whenever the prophetic fathers and mothers are honoring testimonies. But it does not take long until the rest of the prophetic community gets pretty sick of these people. The way out of this for them is twofold. First, you need to confront them privately, as we talked about earlier in this chapter. Second, you need to find healthy attributes to affirm in them so that they are getting the attention they need, while at the same time growing in character.

Another superhero challenge is that often, these people are habitually hyper-spiritual, meaning that they see angels in every corner, Jesus often speaks to them audibly and they frequently have "heavenly experiences." Again, we certainly want to encourage our prophetic people to move in high levels of spiritual anointing, and we do not want to discount the Holy Spirit's ability to use anyone powerfully. But I have found that many of these hyper-spiritual prophetic people actually live in high levels of the fear of reality. They have retreated into a world of fantasy that they can control through their imagination.

The apostle Paul (who himself had heavenly experiences) must have also shepherded people with this syndrome playing out in their lives, because he wrote, "Let no one keep defrauding you of your prize by delighting in self-abasement and the worship of the angels, taking his stand on visions he has seen, inflated without cause by his fleshly mind" (Colossians 2:18). Every person I have ever dealt with who is in this situation has retreated into fantasy because his or her reality was too painful to deal with. They often live in fantasy so long that it becomes a way of life, a way to cope, a way to escape their agony. If this is the case with your superheroes, they do not need to be reprimanded; they need to be healed and restored so that they can live pain-free in the Kingdom.

Identify the superheroes in disguise

There will also be genuine spiritual superheroes who will become key members of your prophetic community. You may need to exercise some careful discernment about who these superheroes are. Their identity will probably surprise you. The funny thing is that they are commonly people whom I would never choose for that role. They may be the socially awkward people, the people who do not have great character or the people who are rather strange.

I know it sounds judgmental when I say that I would not "choose" these people to fill a superhero role, but it just goes to show that God often prefers to use the weak, the weird or the not so good-looking in extraordinary ways. God's choices may differ from what I expect. I am always careful, therefore, not to make quick decisions about what dynamic might be taking place in the superheroes whom God has assigned to my care.

I try to use discernment as I work with these unique people who are superheroes in disguise and help them grow in their gift, in their relationship with God and in their ability to be part of our prophetic community.

Help the fearful get free

A final key I want to mention in building a faith culture involves helping the fearful among you get free. If the fearful are going to accomplish everything God has planned for them, and if your community is going to become as strong and healthy as God intends, this is a necessity. Fearful people are often petrified of being punished, embarrassed or exposed. As prophets and prophetesses, we commonly feel compassion for these people and allow them to retreat into silence. While that is undoubtedly the most comfortable course all around, it is neither healthy for them nor for your prophetic community.

I have discovered that I could never overcome fear in my life by allowing it to dictate my behavior or by letting it tell me what to do. You and I must face our fears to overcome them, so I always proactively go after the fearful. I am patient but unwavering when I pastor them in our prophetic community. I refuse to let them remain silent, become nonparticipants or behave like victims. I do my best to discern what they are afraid of, then I purposely guide that giant into their land and introduce them to it.

For example, one day I was teaching a prophetic training session in our first-year class at the supernatural school. I was randomly choosing people and having them prophesy over some other randomly chosen person in front of the class of a thousand students. One particular young lady in the class was extremely timid, but I could see that she had a great gift on her life. As I walked toward her, she put her head down and tried to ignore me. I asked her to stand up.

She slowly stood, shaking as she straightened up. Feeling her anxiety, the other students became painfully quiet. I chose another student and brought him to her row.

Handing her the microphone, I said, "I want you to sing a prophecy over this young man!"

At first she refused to take the microphone. Weeping, she whispered quietly, "I can't sing . . . I . . . I . . . rea . . . rea . . . really can't sing."

"Sure you can!" I responded confidently, while insisting that she take the microphone.

She grabbed it from me and began to shake violently. She finally collapsed on the ground, sobbing dramatically. "I can't . . . I can't . . . I can't do this!" she insisted.

"Yes, you can! We'll wait while you get a word for him," I persisted.

By now the entire class was moaning their disapproval of my insistence. I honestly felt bad for the young lady, too, but I had a deep sense that I was doing the right thing. She continued to stay on the floor, weeping.

I took the microphone, put it close to her mouth and said, "It's no problem; we have another hour of class. I don't mind waiting, so please don't feel rushed."

Five minutes passed as she lay sobbing into the microphone. Everyone could hear her now, and the class was growing increasingly angry with me. They were beginning to make comments like, "Come on, Pastor, leave her alone."

Ten minutes passed, and by now the young man who was waiting for the prophecy tried to negotiate with me on her behalf.

"I don't really need a prophecy," he said. "It's no problem. She doesn't have to give me a prophecy."

I ignored him and continued to quietly encourage her, "Come on, lady, you can do this. Face your fear! Get up and minister to this man. You really need to do this."

Fifteen minutes passed as she lay motionless on the floor. Her weeping had gone silent, but the student's protests had increased exponentially in the last few minutes. Finally, she slowly made her way to her feet, trembling like a leaf as she stood.

I handed her the microphone again and said softly, "You can do this."

The class started praying quietly as she stood there with her head hanging down and the microphone shaking in her trembling right hand.

A couple more minutes passed, then suddenly, in a squeaky, off-key voice, she sang softly, "Go . . . God lov . . . loves you. He re . . . really, really loves you. And He th . . . thinks you are amazing!"

When she handed me the microphone and plopped into her seat, the class went wild. They spontaneously stood to their feet, clapping and shouting for over five minutes. She sat there with her head in her hands, weeping out loud.

For the next couple weeks, this young woman refused to speak to me or even look at me. I did not really blame her. I could feel her pain. Then one day she waited for me after class and caught me at the door.

"I was really angry with you," she told me frankly. "That was a very painful experience for me," she continued as she looked into my eyes, "but something happened to me on the floor that day . . . something powerful. The fear that has controlled me my entire life broke suddenly. I could feel chains falling off my soul! For the first time ever, I feel alive and free, and I feel like myself. Thank you so much for believing in me and for not allowing me to stay in my fear."

I hugged her and gave her a kiss on the forehead. Later that week she shared her testimony with the entire class, and once again the class went wild! Her victory had become their victory . . . her testimony had become their testimony . . . her courage had inspired them to become courageous.

Over the next several weeks her freedom spread to the entire class as they faced their fears. One by one, they became an unshackled and uninhibited band of sons and daughters. That year we graduated a mighty army of prophetic warriors!

8

STANDING BEFORE KINGS

We in the Body of Christ desperately need to learn how to influence society in such a way that people are drawn to us. This is especially true because we only have as much influence in people's lives as they have value for us. Our failure to disciple nations is largely a manifestation of our lack of understanding about how to bring true transformation to people's lives, especially to those who are not yet hungry for it.

Jesus commissioned us to *make* disciples of *all* nations and then *teach* them (see Matthew 28:18–20). The Greek word for disciple, *mathetes*, means "learner." It may surprise some leaders that we are responsible to *create learners* and then to *teach them.*

I have heard many leaders say things like, "People are just not hungry for the truth." What these leaders do not realize is that we are responsible to motivate people to want to learn, receive and grow so that we can teach, equip and train them. Most of us have had an important person in our life who was so passionate about a particular subject that he or she inspired the same interest in us and caused us to hunger to know more. This is what we are called to do for *all* the nations of the world.

Many people in the world are Gospel intolerant. When they listen to the preaching of the Word, it has no effect on them, or worse yet, it actually creates a negative reaction in some of them. Then there are others who have consumed just enough religion to inoculate them from the real Jesus. Hearing about the Bible without experiencing God leads to religious form without any power (see 2 Timothy 3:5). It is like exchanging the Communion meal for a dinner commentary or a cookbook. We owe the world an encounter with God Himself. When people get exposed to their Creator, they find Him enticing—simply irresistible.

Wisdom Finds a Way

The other night Bill Johnson was sharing on this very subject, and he said, "The Church has learned to answer questions the world isn't asking. This is primarily because we have trained people to answer the questions the world *should be asking!*"

To illustrate his point, Bill went on to tell the story of the prophet Samuel meeting Saul. Saul was looking for his father's lost donkeys, and his servant convinced him to go to the next village, where there was a prophet whom they could ask. They could see if the prophet knew where the donkeys were. Here is the biblical account of Samuel and Saul's exchange:

> Then Saul approached Samuel in the gate and said, "Please tell me where the seer's house is." Samuel answered Saul and said, "I am the seer. Go up before me to the high place,

for you shall eat with me today; and in the morning I will let you go, and will tell you all that is on your mind. As for your donkeys which were lost three days ago, do not set your mind on them, for they have been found. And for whom is all that is desirable in Israel? Is it not for you and for all your father's household?" Saul replied, "Am I not a Benjamite, of the smallest of the tribes of Israel, and my family the least of all the families of the tribe of Benjamin? Why then do you speak to me in this way?"

1 Samuel 9:18–21

The net result of their meeting was this:

Then Samuel took the flask of oil, poured it on his head, kissed him and said, "Has not the LORD anointed you a ruler over His inheritance?"

1 Samuel 10:1

The question Saul should have been asking was, "Who is supposed to be the king of Israel?" But Saul was not asking that question because he was entrenched in the problems of daily life. Chasing donkeys had taken the place of finding his destiny. But God had given the prophet Samuel great wisdom. Samuel answered the question Saul was asking (about the donkeys) so that he had an opportunity to answer the question Saul should have been asking (about the kingship), which ultimately resulted in Samuel commissioning Saul as Israel's king.

Prophets Who Transform Nations

Prophets and prophetesses have a divine call on their lives to help transform nations. But one of the challenging aspects of cultural transformation in the twenty-first century is that most nations do not even acknowledge prophets and prophetesses, much less invite them to speak into their country's destinies. In other words, unlike in the days of Saul, people today are not going to the prophets to get *any* of their questions answered. How, then, do prophets and prophetesses become cultural catalysts that lead to the kingdoms of this world becoming the Kingdom of our God?

This question has literally plagued me for years. But recently the Lord opened my eyes to understand how certain prophets guided Gentile kings into His divine destiny for them even before the cross of Christ. God began to give me revelation into the lives of two prophets in the Old Testament, Joseph and Daniel, who practically and supernaturally altered the history of nations. I was stunned as I considered the impact these two men had on godless and wicked nations.

The other thing that really woke me up to God's incredible ability to use anyone is that both of these men were Israelites imprisoned in a foreign land. Let's look deeper into the history of these two great prophets. My prayer is that their lives would have as much impact on you as they have had on me.

A Supernatural Heritage

Let's begin with the life of Joseph. Joseph was a young man who came from a large, dysfunctional, blended family. His dad had two wives and two mistresses, which ultimately yielded one brother and ten half brothers. Joseph was the eleventh son of Jacob. His father openly favored him because he was the son of his old age, not to mention that Joseph was also one of the two sons of Rachel, the only woman Jacob ever really loved.

This scenario created an atmosphere that inspired intense jealousy among Joseph's brothers. And Joseph, being young and vindictive, responded by constantly tattling on his older brothers. His brothers' jealousy escalated when their father robed Joseph in a multicolored coat that he had made himself by hand.

When Joseph was seventeen years old, he had an amazing dream about his destiny and the fate of his family. With all the dysfunction among his brothers, you would think Joseph would have had the sense to keep the dream to himself. Instead, he used the dream to taunt his brothers.

Joseph said to them, "Please listen to this dream which I have had; for behold, we were binding sheaves in the field, and lo, my sheaf rose up and also stood erect; and behold, your sheaves gathered around and bowed down to my sheaf" (Genesis 37:6–7).

Joseph's brothers responded predictably, yet insightfully: "Then his brothers said to him, 'Are you actually going to reign over us? Or are you really going to rule over us?' So they hated him even more for his dreams and for his words" (verse 8).

Joseph had never said a word about ruling over his brothers; he had simply shared his dream with them. But the implications were clear to them. A few nights later Joseph dreamt again, and he seemed determined to mock his brothers with his revelation. In essence, he said, "Hey guys, I had another dream. Let me tell you about it. In the dream, I saw the sun and the moon and eleven stars all bowing down to me" (see verse 9).

This only served to further escalate his brothers' hatred for him. He went on to share the dream with his father.

When his dad heard it, he rebuked Joseph and said to him, "What is this dream that you have had? Shall I and your mother and your brothers actually come to bow ourselves down before you to the ground?" (verse 10).

It is important to remember here that Joseph had never said anything about his brothers, father or mother serving him, either. He had simply related a dream about the sun, moon and stars bowing down to him. But Joseph was born into a legacy of dream interpreters and prophets. His father, Jacob, was famous for experiencing angel encounters and open visions. Jacob's entire family understood the spirit world and the language of God. Interpreting dreams was second nature for Joseph because he was born into a supernatural family. Although his family was relationally dysfunctional, they were spiritually intuitive, so Joseph had a supernatural heritage to begin with.

Just as a side note, I think that kind of supernatural heritage is a rare thing these days. Do you remember how I mentioned in chapter 2 that when Jesus died on the cross, it was a fulfillment of the prophet Joel's words that the sun would turn dark and the moon would turn to blood? (See Acts 2:15–21.) I described in some detail how the sun represented the Father and the moon represented Jesus. Those Scriptures were written in a spiritually intuitive culture where people understood the language of the Spirit. But the challenge today is that the Bible is often interpreted and translated by theologians who are prone to take a cerebral approach to God and who are ignorant of this symbolic kind of hieroglyphic language. Approaching the Scriptures cerebrally often leads to all kinds of strange conclusions about the author's intentions.

The Tangible Favor of God

Let's get back to Joseph's story. Not long after all this drama took place with his family, Joseph's father sent him to check on his brothers, who were in another village shepherding a flock of sheep. When his brothers saw him off in the distance, they hatched a plot to kill him. Thankfully his oldest brother, Reuben, was not quite as vindictive as the rest. Reuben convinced them to spare Joseph's life and throw him into a pit. Meanwhile, a bunch of Ishmaelite slave traders passed by, so his brothers pulled him out of the pit and sold him into slavery for twenty pieces of silver.

By the time his brothers got back to the house of Jacob, they had covered Joseph's multicolored coat in animal blood to convince his father that a wild beast had killed him. While Jacob mourned his son's supposed death, the Ishmaelites sold Joseph in Egypt. His new master was Potiphar, an officer of Pharaoh and the captain of his bodyguard. Genesis gives us an account of Joseph's life as a slave:

> The LORD was with Joseph, so he became a successful man. And he was in the house of his master, the Egyptian. Now his master saw that the LORD was with him and how the LORD caused all that he did to prosper in his hand. So Joseph found favor in his sight and became his personal servant; and he made him overseer over his house, and all that he owned he put in his charge. It came about that from the time he made him overseer in his house and over all that he owned, the LORD blessed the Egyptian's house on account of Joseph; thus the LORD's blessing was upon all that he owned, in the house and in the field. So he left everything he owned in Joseph's charge; and with him there he did not concern himself with anything except the food which he ate.
>
> Genesis 39:2–6

This story is powerful, yet it is also somewhat ironic in that God blessed the leader who enslaved Joseph because of the favor on Joseph's life. Furthermore, the slave owner put Joseph in charge of *everything* he owned because he could "see" that God—the God he did not know—was with Joseph. This inspires all kinds of questions in my mind. For instance, what did Potiphar actually see in Joseph? What part of God's presence became tangible enough for an Egyptian leader who did not believe in God to actually trust with his heart what he could not possibly understand with his head?

It suffices to say here that if we as prophets and prophetesses are going to be part of a team that transforms the world, it is vital that we tap in to the tangible favor of God the way Joseph did. Jesus put it like this: "Let your light shine before men in such a way that they may see your good works, and glorify your Father who is in heaven" (Matthew 5:16).

Unfortunately, Joseph's glory days at Potiphar's house did not end well because Potiphar's wife was a seductive adulteress and a ruthless liar. After Joseph bravely and virtuously refused her sexual advances, she convinced her husband that Joseph was trying to rape her. Without so much as a trial, Joseph's master sent him to prison for rape. This is where the plot thickens, because the prison Joseph went to happened to be the place where all the political prisoners were sentenced by Pharaoh.

I am not exactly sure how you can view a prisoner as a successful man, yet that is how God saw Joseph. Take a close look at the Genesis account of his jail time:

> The LORD was with Joseph and extended kindness to him, and gave him favor in the sight of the chief jailer. The chief jailer committed to Joseph's charge all the prisoners who were in the jail; so that whatever was done there, he was responsible for it. The chief jailer did not supervise anything under Joseph's charge because the LORD was with him; and whatever he did, the LORD made to prosper.
>
> Genesis 39:21–23

Soon after Joseph became overseer of the jail, Pharaoh threw his chief cupbearer and chief baker both into a cell that was under Joseph's supervision. After some time went by, both officials had a dream on the same night. Joseph, being the ever-so-discerning one, realized that his two friends were troubled and inquired about why they had such fallen countenances. This resulted in both men relating their dreams to Joseph, who, of course, had grown up with a supernatural heritage in a house of dream interpreters.

After hearing the cupbearer's dream, Joseph told him the dream meant that "within three more days Pharaoh will lift up your head and restore you to your office; and you will put Pharaoh's cup into his hand according to your former custom when you were his cupbearer" (Genesis 40:13).

When the chief baker saw that Joseph had interpreted his co-worker's dream favorably, he told Joseph his dream as well. This time, the interpretation was a different story.

Joseph answered the chief baker, "The three baskets are three days; within three more days Pharaoh will lift up your head from you and will hang you on a tree, and the birds will eat your flesh off you" (verses 18–19).

Joseph was right. Three days later, the cupbearer was restored to his office of serving Pharaoh, while the chief baker was hung for treason.

At the time that he interpreted their dreams, Joseph had begged the cupbearer to use his influence with Pharaoh to free him from prison. But when the cupbearer was restored to his position, he completely forgot about Joseph. Two long years passed, and finally Pharaoh had a dream that no one could interpret. Pharaoh's dream jogged his cupbearer's memory so that he related to Pharaoh that Joseph had accurately interpreted two dreams in prison. (Better late than never, I

SCHOOL OF THE PROPHETS

guess!) Immediately Pharaoh called for Joseph's release so that Joseph could interpret his dreams.

They cleaned Joseph up and took him to the palace, and when he arrived before the ruler of all Egypt, Pharaoh said to him, "I have had a dream, but no one can interpret it; and I have heard it said about you, that when you hear a dream you can interpret it" (Genesis 41:15).

Right away, Joseph started talking about the favor of God. He answered Pharaoh, "It is not in me; God will give Pharaoh a favorable answer" (verse 16).

Pharaoh related his dream to Joseph, telling him about the seven sleek, fat cows whom he saw being devoured by the seven ugly, lean cows, and about the seven full, good ears of corn he saw being swallowed up by the withered, scorched ears (see Genesis 41:17–24). Joseph interpreted the dream as meaning that seven years of abundance in Egypt would be used up by seven years of severe famine. Then he advised Pharaoh about what to do about it in response:

> Now let Pharaoh look for a man discerning and wise, and set him over the land of Egypt. Let Pharaoh take action to appoint overseers in charge of the land, and let him exact a fifth of the produce of the land of Egypt in the seven years of abundance. Then let them gather all the food of these good years that are coming, and store up the grain for food in the cities under Pharaoh's authority, and let them guard it. Let the food become as a reserve for the land for the seven years of famine which will occur in the land of Egypt, so that the land will not perish during the famine.
>
> Genesis 41:33–36

Pharaoh was so moved by Joseph's dream interpretations and his wise strategy to save Egypt that he immediately promoted Joseph as leader over all Egypt. The account is so stunning that I think it is worth relating in its entirety. Look at this amazing moment of Joseph's promotion:

> Then Pharaoh said to his servants, "Can we find a man like this, in whom is a divine spirit?" So Pharaoh said to Joseph, "Since God has informed you of all this, there is no one so discerning and wise as you are. You shall be over my house, and according to your command all my people shall do homage; only in the throne I will be greater than you." Pharaoh said to Joseph, "See, I have set you over all the land of Egypt." Then Pharaoh took off his signet ring from his hand and put it on Joseph's hand, and clothed him in garments of fine linen and put the gold necklace around his neck. He had him ride in his second chariot; and they proclaimed before him, "Bow the knee!" And he set him over all the land of Egypt. Moreover, Pharaoh said to Joseph, "Though I am Pharaoh, yet without your permission no one shall raise his hand or foot in all the land of Egypt."
>
> Genesis 41:38–44

Pharaoh went on to name Joseph Zaphenath-paneah, which means "God speaks and He lives!" From that point, all kinds of interesting things happened. Pharaoh also gave Joseph Asenath, the daughter of Potiphera priest of On, as his wife. God used this marriage to strengthen Joseph's new position as a national leader. The city of On was also known as "the City of the Sun." It was the center of worship of the sun god, Ra. The high priest in On held the title of "Greatest of Seers." When Joseph married into this family, he joined a social class befitting a national leader.

Also implied in the marriage arrangement was Pharaoh's confidence that Joseph, too, was a "seer" or prophet of the highest caliber. It is likewise interesting to note that although Joseph basically married into a cult, his wife bore him two sons, Manasseh and Ephraim, who became two tribes in Israel.

Fathering Nations

Nine long years passed, and the famine began to ravage the nations. The Israelites were starving to death, so Jacob sent ten of his sons into Egypt because he heard a rumor that there was food there. Through a series of circumstances Joseph encountered his brothers, who were trying to purchase food in Egypt. He disguised himself and worked out a plan to make them bring Benjamin, his younger brother whom he had never met, back to Egypt.

When his brothers returned the second time with Benjamin, Joseph was beside himself. Weeping uncontrollably, he sent all the Egyptians out of the room. Then Joseph said to his brothers, "I am Joseph! Is my father still alive?" (Genesis 45:3).

Understandably, his brothers were so dismayed by this revelation that they could not answer him, so Joseph continued,

> I am your brother Joseph, whom you sold into Egypt. Now do not be grieved or angry with yourselves, because you sold me here, for God sent me before you to preserve life. For the famine has been in the land these two years, and there are still five years in which there will be neither plowing nor harvesting. God sent me before you to preserve for you a remnant in the earth, and to keep you alive by a great deliverance.
>
> Genesis 45:4–7

Then Joseph made one of the most powerful statements in the entire Old Testament when he said to his brothers, "It was not you who sent me here, but God; and He has made me a father to Pharaoh" (verse 8).

Joseph is not only leading a nation; he is fathering Pharaoh! Joseph is a great example of a prophet who fathered a nation. Although he was born in Israel and therefore was not technically an Egyptian, yet he became one of them through his love for the people. Fathering nations was a promise God made to Abraham, who is the father of our faith and a prophet of God. Speaking of Abraham, the Bible calls him this:

> . . . the father of us all, (as it is written, "A father of many nations have I made you") in the presence of Him whom he believed, even God, who gives life to the dead and calls into being that which does not exist. In hope against hope he [Abraham] believed, so that he might become a father of many nations according to that which had been spoken, "So shall your descendants be."
>
> Romans 4:16–18

Contrary to popular opinion, Abraham was not an Israelite. There were no Israelites until Jacob was born and his name was changed to Israel. Neither was Abraham Jewish, because the Jewish people came from Judah, who was one of the twelve tribes of Israel. (All Jewish people are Israelis, but not all Israelis are Jewish.) Abraham is the father of many nations, just as Scripture says. He was not a fatherly ambassador whom God sent *to* nations to represent Him. Instead, Abraham was a father *of* many nations. In other words, his spiritual ethnic origin was global, not Jewish.

The story of Joseph teaches us that there is a huge difference between being a prophet *to the nations* and being a prophet *of the nations*. Prophesying internationally and helping be a voice to the nations is an important ministry, but becoming a prophet of a nation or nations requires the nations to embrace us as fathers or mothers and not to view us as outsiders looking in. Simply put, we must become one of them. This requires us to understand their global perspectives, respect their views and then help shape them prophetically from the inside out.

Israel Meets Pharaoh

The divine partnership between Joseph and Pharaoh is absolutely intriguing. It demonstrates God's ability to orchestrate relationships on a level that is not only fascinating and encouraging, but is also incredibly insightful. The concept that Joseph and Pharaoh were actually partners in destiny is mind-boggling. Think about it: Joseph had a dream about being a great ruler, and Pharaoh had a dream about the destiny of his country. Without Joseph's dream, Pharaoh and all Egypt would have perished in a famine. But it is equally true that if Pharaoh would not have dreamt, Joseph would have died in prison, and his vision of being a great ruler would have died with him. (Although this is a side note, I think it is worth mentioning that commonly young men like Joseph tend to dream about themselves, while rulers like Pharaoh dream about the welfare of their countries.)

The fact that Pharaoh chose a prisoner whom he had never met before to rule his country speaks of the mastery of God to so instill His favor inside someone that even those who do not know God are inspired to promote him or her. The story of Joseph and Pharaoh is probably one of the most profound aspects of the history of their two countries. Egypt was just one generation away from becoming Israel's oppressor, because of which God would need to raise up a deliverer named Moses to set His people free from a wicked pharaoh who enslaved them. Thousands of years later, that infamous pharaoh and Egypt itself would be used as prophetic and symbolic metaphors for the salvation experience. Jesus delivered us from the pharaoh of this world (the devil), led us out of the land of Egypt (bondage), baptized us in the Red Sea (saved us), took us through the wilderness (we left our old man there) and finally gave us the Promised Land (we entered the Kingdom of God).

Of course, in this prophetic metaphor Israel is often used as the symbol of the Church and/or of believers who have escaped the clutches of pharaoh. Remember how the Israelites had to put the blood of a spotless lamb over the doorpost of their houses so the death angel would pass over them? This story is not just a great preachers' metaphor, it is the hand of God painting the story of salvation in the sands of time through the history of Egypt and Israel.

Maybe even more powerful is the way Egypt represents the world that is corrupt and without God, while Jacob and Joseph—because they were sons of Abraham, the father of faith, and they lived four hundred years before the law of Moses—represent the people of God who are blessed by faith and are living in the favor they have received by grace (not by works).

I took the time to remind you of all this metaphorical meaning because of what is about to happen next in Joseph's story and the prophetic impact it should have on prophets and prophetesses. Joseph brings his father and seventy of his family members into Egypt to escape the famine. Then Joseph does something profound. He introduces Jacob/Israel to the pharaoh of Egypt. Read the stunning account for yourself:

> Then Joseph brought his father Jacob and presented him to Pharaoh; and Jacob *blessed* Pharaoh. Pharaoh said to Jacob, "How many years have you lived?" So Jacob said to Pharaoh, "The years of my sojourning are one hundred and thirty; few and unpleasant have been the years of my life, nor have they attained the years that my fathers lived during the days of their sojourning." And Jacob *blessed* Pharaoh, and went out from his presence. So Joseph settled his father and his brothers and gave them a possession in the land of Egypt,

in the best of the land, in the land of Rameses, as Pharaoh had ordered.

Genesis 47:7–11, emphasis added

I hope you caught what just happened. Jacob *blessed* Pharaoh. If God is using Jacob and Pharaoh as metaphors for the way that the Church relates to the world, then we must take note of this profound act that took place in Egypt. This is the divine key to transforming nations, the combination lock to an untouchable world, the open door to making disciples of all nations.

But wait, it gets even better. Pharaoh was so taken by Joseph and Jacob's love that he gave them the best land in all of Egypt. What kind of metaphor might that be regarding today's relationship between the world we live in and the prophets and prophetesses of our time?

Seventeen years later, when Jacob/Israel was 147 years old and the time for him to die drew near, he called his son Joseph and told him, "Please do not bury me in Egypt, but when I lie down with my fathers, you shall carry me out of Egypt and bury me in their burial place" (Genesis 47:29–30).

Joseph promised him, "I will do as you have said," and Jacob asked, "Swear to me," so Joseph swore it to him (verses 30–31).

Soon after this, Israel (Jacob) blessed all his sons and both of Joseph's sons and breathed his last. Joseph fell on his father's face and wept over him and kissed him. Then Joseph commanded his servants the physicians to embalm his father. It took them forty days to embalm him, *but* the Egyptians wept for him seventy days.

I hope you are getting this. It was not the Israelites who wept; it was the Egyptians!

Joseph had to get permission from Pharaoh to bury Israel in the land of Canaan, as he had sworn he would do. When

Joseph finally mustered up the courage to ask Pharaoh's permission, Pharaoh's immediate response was, "Go up and bury your father, as he made you swear" (Genesis 50:6).

When Joseph left Egypt, a procession of the servants of Pharaoh, the elders of his household and all the elders of the land of Egypt went with him. Both chariots and horsemen also went with him, "a very great company" (verse 9). At the threshing floor of Atad beyond the Jordan, in the land of Canaan, they lamented "with a very great and sorrowful lamentation" (verse 10).

When the Canaanites saw the mourning, they said, "This is a grievous mourning for the Egyptians" (verse 11), so they named the place Abel-mizraim, which means "the meadow where the Egyptians mourned."

This entire story inspires so many questions in me. What if the prophets and prophetesses of God became like Joseph, who so blessed Pharaoh and Egypt that all Egypt literally grieved for him when his father passed away? Would our blessing on the world and its peoples evoke so much response from them?

Remember, this all happened in the Old Testament, long before the cross of Christ quenched the fires of judgment and transferred us to the mercy seat. Ask yourself what is keeping the prophets of God from befriending the pharaohs of this present world and helping them avoid famines and become successful leaders. What is keeping the prophets of today from blessing the world the way Israel blessed Pharaoh?

Different Times, Stunning Similarities

Nearly nine hundred years later, and almost a thousand miles away, another prophet was taken captive by a radically more wicked king than the pharaoh Joseph served. The famous king of Babylon, Nebuchadnezzar, destroyed Israel, tore down the Temple of Solomon and took the prophet Daniel captive, along with many others.

The number of similarities between Joseph and Daniel is stunning. Both of them were Israelite slaves who rose to power through the gift of dream interpretation. Much like the prophet Joseph, who refused to have sex with his master's wife, Daniel also lived according to godly virtues. For instance, Daniel refused to defile himself with the king's wine and choice food (see Daniel 1:8), and he insisted on praying three times a day by kneeling toward Jerusalem (see Daniel 6:10). Joseph married into the cultic family of On, while Daniel became the chief of the magicians (see Daniel 5:11). In fact, Daniel so assimilated into the Babylonian culture that he even took on the name of a Babylonian god. His name was changed to Belteshazzar, which was the name of Nebuchadnezzar's god (see Daniel 4:8).

Both these prophets managed to culturalize their lives so that they could meet the needs of the evil empires in which they resided without compromising their character. (Though it does seem odd to me that Daniel would not eat the king's food, but became the chief magician and allowed four kings to think of him as a cultist.) When Daniel first arrived in Babylon as a captive, Nebuchadnezzar ordered Daniel's overseer to teach him "the literature and language of the Chaldeans" for three years (Daniel 1:4). This helped him assimilate into the Chaldean culture and learn the language of Babylon. Joseph also grew up in a foreign culture, having been sold into slavery in Egypt as a young man. He learned the ways of Egypt and spoke their language, eventually reaching the very courts of Pharaoh.

The favor of God on Joseph and Daniel's lives caused both

of them trouble among their peers. Joseph's brothers were so jealous of him that they wanted to kill him, while Daniel was thrown into the lions' den because of a plot carried out by his fellow conjurers, who envied him desperately and hated him passionately.

Another striking similarity between these two prophets was their ability to forgive. Joseph forgave his brothers who sold him into slavery, telling them that what they meant for evil God meant for good. Daniel forgave Nebuchadnezzar, who had destroyed his country and probably had killed his family. In neither case was this passive forgiveness for some small offense. Instead, these two men chose to live their lives in a way that would benefit the people who had tried to destroy them.

In addition, Joseph and Daniel both had an extraordinary gift of government on their lives. They not only prophesied to the kings they served; they also had supernatural wisdom from God available, and they accessed it to guide nations into their God-given destinies.

Probably the most striking resemblance between these two great prophets, however, is that they *loved* the people whom they served. I believe that is most likely the ultimate reason why God gave them such tremendous access to such powerful kings. A gut-level honest, "I have no agenda" kind of love like the Father's exuded from both these men. This love became contagious and resulted in their kings loving them passionately. I already shared with you how much Joseph was loved by Pharaoh, who gave him and his family the best of the land. And we saw how all the Egyptians wept when Joseph's father, Jacob, died.

Daniel and the kings he served had the same kind of love for one another. When Nebuchadnezzar had a horrible dream about losing his mind and his kingdom, Daniel was so distressed by it that he did not want to interpret the dream because of its negative connotations for the king he loved. The Bible records the incident:

> Then Daniel, whose name is Belteshazzar, was appalled for a while as his thoughts alarmed him. The king responded and said, "Belteshazzar, do not let the dream or its interpretation alarm you." Belteshazzar replied, "My lord, if only the dream applied to those who hate you and its interpretation to your adversaries!"
>
> Daniel 4:19

The man who destroyed Daniel's country, tore down his beloved Temple and led him and his family into captivity was finally about to get what he deserved. But when Daniel the prophet heard the dream and the king pressed him for the interpretation, Daniel responded, "I wish this dream was about those who hate you!"

Many years later, when Daniel was about ninety years old, he served a Persian king named Darius. The other government officials tricked Darius into throwing Daniel into the lions' den. But Darius and Daniel loved one another. Here is the account:

> Then the king went off to his palace and spent the night fasting, and no entertainment was brought before him; and his sleep fled from him.
>
> Then the king arose at dawn, at the break of day, and went in haste to the lions' den. When he had come near the den to Daniel, he cried out with a troubled voice. The king spoke and said to Daniel, "Daniel, servant of the living God, has your God, whom you constantly serve, been able to deliver you from the lions?" Then Daniel spoke to the king, "O king, live forever! My God sent His angel and shut the lions' mouths and they have not harmed me, inasmuch as I was

found innocent before Him; and also toward you, O king, I
have committed no crime."

Daniel 6:18–22

How does a prophet find so much love for a king who just
threw him into the lions' den that he can say to him, "O King,
live forever"? And why does a powerful king fast all night for
an old Jewish prophet, then run to the lions' den early in the
morning and shout, "Has your God, whom you constantly
serve, been able to deliver you from the lions?"

Mine are honest questions: Why all the drama? Why all the
passion? *Why?* That is the real question. What prompted five
Gentile kings to befriend two foreign prophets and promote
them to the pinnacle of their kingdoms?

Before you try to answer, we need to investigate one more
king. His name was Cyrus. King Cyrus the Great was the last
in a long line of rulers whom Daniel served. Although Daniel
was quite old when he worked for Cyrus, his influence on that
particular king might well be Daniel's greatest legacy. Not only
is Cyrus credited with the release and restoration of the Israelis,
which he funded entirely from his own treasury, but he is also
the father of the concept of human rights. Twenty-five hundred
years ago, King Cyrus authored what is now called the first
human rights charter, which has become the prototype for the
United Nations. Literally billons of people owe their freedom
and equality to a Persian king whose rule was prophesied by
Isaiah and Jeremiah years before he was born (see Isaiah 45:1–7;
Ezra 1:1). This extraordinary man was guarded by angels and
mentored by the prophet Daniel (see Daniel 10).

From the opening scenes of these prophets' stories, Joseph
and Daniel's great character, supernatural powers and extraordinary love continually exposed the Egyptians, Babylonians and Persians to the superior realm of God's Kingdom.

My Call

Like Joseph and Daniel, God has called me as a prophetic father not just *to the nations*, but as a father *of many nations*. Like Joseph and Daniel, I must therefore become one of them so that I can lead, father, equip and protect the nations I am called to father. It is also therefore necessary that I learn the ways and the language of Egypt and Babylon, so to speak.

Although I am an intensely patriotic American, I have to learn how to embrace a sense of belonging to every nation that God has called me to father. I cannot allow my American perspectives to undermine the call of God on my life to be loyal to other nations as well. Nor can I let my American patriotism undermine my ability to understand the cultural perspectives and global insights of the other nations I am fathering.

I realize, however, that I must navigate my situation with extreme wisdom so that I remain loyal, dedicated and responsible to my own country first. Yet these international sons and daughters of mine have a very different outlook on our country's place in history than we Americans do. It is important for me to acknowledge that. Otherwise, black-and-white thinking and "good guy, bad guy," "us and them" perspectives could keep me from understanding the root system behind the way those in other countries think and therefore behave.

For instance, we Americans tend to see ourselves as the "good guys," doing our best to bring about truth, justice and the American way. We believe that extending democracy to the nations is sort of our mission from God. We tend to view any country that opposes or disagrees with democracy as bad, or at least not as advanced as we are.

I am not trying to diminish democracy, nor am I trying to make a case for it. I am simply acknowledging that I see the world through American core values. The challenge is that I often mistake my American core values for Kingdom core values because I was raised to believe that we as United States citizens are always right; therefore everyone who disagrees with us must be wrong.

As I travel the world, though, I have come to realize that every country views world history through its own core perspectives. For instance, we Americans and the Japanese have very different perspectives on the Second World War, especially when it comes to events such as the bombing of Hiroshima and Nagasaki. I am sure that history classes in Japan and America teach these same events from widely different viewpoints.

Another example I have recently been exposed to is the way in which many of the Russian people view the KGB. Russians do not necessarily view members of the KGB as bad people, although they understand that many KGB members committed atrocities. But most Russians will not group them all in the same category and label them as bad. When a former KGB person runs for office or holds a particular position in Russia, the people do not view them through the eyes of "guilt by association." They see them as being drafted into a duty for their country in a time of war and international opposition. They acknowledge that many (though not all) KGB members felt as though they had no choice except to serve their country in the way that they did. But because many members of the KGB committed terrible crimes against people, they are all scorned in countries like America as being inherently evil.

From a global perspective, there are no real good guys in war, although most would acknowledge that there were, and are, bad guys like Adolf Hitler. In reality, however, we find that most of our heroes are flawed and all of our villains were created in the image of God.

If we are going to be prophets and prophetesses of the nations, then we had better realize that the world is a much more complicated and complex place than we probably ever imagined. It is more difficult to know right from wrong when you view things from a multinational perspective. Because of that, we have a deep need for the Holy Spirit to lead us into all truth. Without the Holy Spirit's direction, our perspectives would be tainted by our national prejudice, dogmatic core values and the influence of media on us. This would render us ineffective as fathers and mothers of other nations.

All Rise

I love overt ministry—the bold preaching of the Gospel, standing in the streets for justice and living out loud. But for me and for the movement I lead, the season has changed. Jesus said it best: "The kingdom of heaven is like leaven, which a woman took and hid in three pecks of flour until it was all leavened" (Matthew 13:33). As he did with Daniel and Joseph, God is kneading His prophets like yeast into the dough of society, so that the entire culture will rise.

Jesus also said, "Behold, I send you out as sheep in the midst of wolves; so be shrewd as serpents and innocent as doves" (Matthew 10:16). God is calling our prophetic movement to be as wise as serpents and as innocent as doves. He is covertly and strategically placing us among high-level influencers so that we can guide the destiny of cities and nations into His divine plan.

A few years ago when I was flying home from another country, I had an amazing experience that drove this revelation of a new season deep into my heart. Just as I was falling asleep, I heard the Lord say to me,

> The season has changed, and it requires a new prophetic mascot. The prophetic mascot for this hour is no longer the eagle; it's the owl. The owl is nocturnal, so it was designed to live in the night, see through the darkness and knows who's who. It is the symbol of wisdom, and it feasts on rats, rodents and snakes.

Wow! I thought to myself. *The occult often uses the owl as a demonic symbol for its counterfeit ministry.*

Then I remembered that God created the owl; the devil was not its creator. I also reminded myself of the days of Daniel and Joseph, prophets with alias names who were hidden in the palaces of kings. Once again, as in the days of Joseph and Daniel, God is strategically placing His prophets and prophetesses—who are filled with love, endowed with wisdom and who walk in great power—into the darkest palaces on the planet. We have been commissioned to enlighten the darkness, be a guide to the blind and bring healing to the nations. This is our call, our mission and our mandate. May God give us grace to expose every world leader to our magnificent King.

It Takes All Kinds

It takes all kinds of prophets to make the world go round. We have taken a lot of time to discuss the covert ministry of Joseph and Daniel in this chapter because, as I mentioned earlier, these two prophets represent the way in which God has called Bethel's prophetic movement to influence the world. In other words, I see the DNA of Joseph and Daniel in our own company of prophets. But I think it is important for us to realize that there are other prophetic models besides Joseph and Daniel in the Scriptures, and these other prophetic models are just as vital for the transformation of culture. Given the scope of this book, I want to briefly mention six models I see (though there are many more). Looking at the differences in these models will help us make sure we do not put God in a certain "prophet box" and miss the greater revelation of His prophetic nature.

- Moses, Eli, Samuel, Deborah and David were all prophets or prophetesses who led their countries. They did not serve national leaders; they *were* the leaders of their countries. Today, as in this model from the past, God is raising up many prophets and prophetesses to lead their cities, countries, companies and organizations.

- The prophets Daniel and Joseph had great relationships with kings and also had a leadership gift to help govern the countries of the leaders whom they served. We have spent a lot of time talking about these two prophets and their prophetic model of being fathers of nations. As I told you, both personally and in my prophetic ministry I relate very closely to this model.

- Two prophets named Nathan and Gad served King David. They both had a great relationship with their king. But for the most part, they only helped to direct David's personal life prophetically and did not assist him in governing their country. That is a stark contrast between these two prophets and Joseph and Daniel. Many prophets and prophetesses are called to disciple political leaders personally, yet they have no prophetic insight into the governmental realm whatsoever. These prophetic people indirectly have a profound impact on the world, even though they may never give their leaders directional words concerning those leaders' realm of authority in governing a country.

- Elijah and Elisha represent a completely different kind of relationship with world leaders. They stood outside the palace, so to speak, and for the most part they had an adversarial relationship with the kings of their nation. Unlike Daniel and Joseph, who served unbelieving Gentile leaders, or Nathan and Gad, who served a man after God's heart, these two prophets had a confrontational relationship with the unrighteous kings of their day. Although today these types of prophets must still embrace the core values of the New Covenant, they are also still called to stand against injustice and to speak up for the sake of righteousness. This can manifest in protests, demonstrations or other public or private calls to holiness. Martin Luther King Jr. would be a good example of a New Testament Elijah or Elisha.

- Hosea and Amos are interesting prophetic types in that they seem to have had no relationship with their country's leadership. These two prophets prophesied to the people and in that way had a secondary effect on their national leaders. They were grassroots prophets who had a dramatic impact on the mindset of the Israeli people. These prophets remind me of many leaders in the Jesus People movement. The Jesus People affected their culture by creating momentum through a righteous prophetic movement of countercultural radicals.

- Jonah was famous for being an unwilling prophet to the unbelieving country of Nineveh. He was kind of the John the Baptist of his day, calling people to repentance for their sins. Although Jonah is an Old Testament prophet, he represents the prophets and prophetesses of today who have an evangelistic mantle for the lost. In my mind, the late David Wilkerson carried this mantle. Although I did not agree with many of David's negative prophetic declarations over our nation, yet at the same time, I recognize that David Wilkerson was a prophet to the unsaved.

As you can see, I did not mention many of the major Old Testament prophets like Isaiah, Ezekiel, Jeremiah, Malachi and several more. Many of them would not fit into the six categories I just mentioned. They were representatives of even more diverse prophetic models. My goal here is that we embrace and honor prophetic diversity. We especially need to honor prophets and prophetesses who carry a different DNA than we do and who have a different call on them than we might have on our lives.

John the Baptist and Jesus

A high value for prophetic diversity began to grow in me a couple of years ago, when I was confronted with my prejudice toward a particular prophetic movement that was trying to influence a culture from outside the king's palace, metaphorically speaking. Much like Mordecai in the book of Esther, who exhorted Esther from outside the castle walls to take a stand for her people, these prophets were shouting their prophecies at our political leaders. They were bold and brash in their prophetic delivery, and they refused to use any form of diplomacy whatsoever.

Having spent years carefully building relationships with high-level influencers around the world, I found myself becoming quite judgmental of these prophets and their mode of operation that is so unlike my own. Then one time, I woke up in the middle of the night with the deep sense that I was to contrast the prophetic ministry of John the Baptist with the ministry of Jesus. To my surprise, a profound revelation started to emerge. It began with the prophecies given to Zacharias, John's father, before John was born. The angel Gabriel told Zacharias regarding John: "For he will be great in the sight of the Lord; and he will drink no wine or liquor, and he will be filled with the Holy Spirit while yet in his mother's womb" (Luke 1:15). Later on, when John began his ministry, he preached a message of radical repentance and railed against sinners. And John the Baptist spoke in the wilderness, wore camel's hair and ate locusts and wild honey (see Mark 1:4–6).

Jesus, on the other hand, hung out with sinners. He wore an expensive, seamless garment and ministered in the Temple and in the synagogues. The first miracle He performed just happened to be making wine for people who were already drunk (see John 2:1–11; 19:23). The contrast between John the Baptist and Jesus was so profound that Jesus actually addressed it Himself. He said,

> For John the Baptist has come eating no bread and drinking no wine, and you say, "He has a demon!" The Son of Man has come eating and drinking, and you say, "Behold, a gluttonous man and a drunkard, a friend of tax collectors and sinners!"
>
> Luke 7:33–34

John's ministry and Jesus' ministry were so diverse that the disciples of John did not think Jesus' disciples were very spiritual, and they actually complained to Jesus about it. They asked Him, "Why do we and the Pharisees fast, but Your disciples do not fast?" (Matthew 9:14).

I was already beginning to see an incredible contrast between these two ministries, but what the Lord showed me next had the greatest impact on me. Matthew describes the scene like this:

Then Jesus arrived from Galilee at the Jordan coming to John, to be baptized by him. But John tried to prevent Him, saying, "I have need to be baptized by You, and do You come to me?" But Jesus answering said to him, "Permit it at this time; for in this way it is fitting for us to fulfill all righteousness." Then he permitted Him. After being baptized, Jesus came up immediately from the water; and behold, the heavens were opened, and he saw the Spirit of God descending as a dove and lighting on Him, and behold, a voice out of the heavens said, "This is My beloved Son, in whom I am well-pleased."

Matthew 3:13–17

Think about what just happened—John's baptism is a baptism of repentance. Jesus never sinned; therefore, He did not need John's baptism. Why did He require John to baptize Him?

Great question! Jesus was baptized to honor the call on John the Baptist's life and to acknowledge the validity of John's polar-opposite ministry. It was only after honoring John that the Holy Spirit came on Jesus and the Father expressed His pleasure to Him. It was John's baptism of Him that launched Jesus into His supernatural ministry.

It is likewise important to note that although Jesus said that "among those born of women there is no one greater than John" (Luke 7:28), John the Baptist did not perform a single recorded miracle.

Jesus, again on the other hand, did so many miracles that the apostle John said, "There are also many other things which Jesus did, which if they were written in detail, I suppose that even the world itself would not contain the books that would be written" (John 21:25).

I want to close this chapter by saying that it takes all kinds of prophets to transform the world, and honor is the high way for us to take in response. It is the high road we need to walk. I have come to understand that it is only when we embrace God's prophetic diversity that we are launched into the "highway" of heavenly power. The world is waiting to see the love of the Father expressed through the power of the prophets and prophetesses—those whose ministries are enhanced by the manifold wisdom of God, who embrace one another in the unity of the Spirit and who are propelled by the bond of peace.

9

NOBLE PROPHETS

We climbed about fifty marble steps leading to two large, ornate doors with huge pillars standing erect on both sides. The heavy doors opened to a breathtaking lobby surrounded with more marble pillars that supported a half-dome, golden cathedral ceiling. My translator and I, dressed up in suits and ties, were greeted by the nation's Secret Service and were led into a room where they would search and interview us. The security officers were businesslike but honorable as they questioned me through my translator about the purpose of my visit. I told them that I was here to meet with the senior member of their government, and I let them know that we had an appointment. (I used the senior official's name with them but have left it out here to hide the identity of this leader and his country. I also changed some of the details of this story, but the story itself is true.)

A few moments later, we were seated in a large, incredibly beautiful room with about thirty-foot-high ceilings. There was a long, rectangular table in the middle of the room that looked as if it could seat forty people.

My translator leaned over to me and whispered nervously, "Do you have a prophetic word for the leader yet?"

"Not yet, but don't worry, I will get a word for him," I responded, trying to comfort my worried companion.

We were whispering to one another, but our words echoed off the stone floors and high ornate ceilings, making it sound as though we were shouting from a mountaintop into a canyon.

Six months earlier, something tremendous had happened that had prepared me ahead of time for such moments. I had met with Cindy Jacobs, founder with her husband, Mike, of Generals International, and I had told her about the call of God on my life to minister to the leaders of nations. I went on to explain that my problem was that I never get any prophetic words for them. Cindy has been ministering to political leaders for years, so I knew she would have some insight into my challenge.

Cindy looked me in the eyes when we met and said, "I never get prophetic words for political leaders until they get into the room!"

That simple key unlocked an entire world for me, and Cindy's words imparted grace to me to minister to political leaders. From that moment on, I never felt any anxiety in the presence of even the most powerful world leaders. I knew that God had called me into this realm and therefore had equipped me with a special grace that gave me supernatural faith for the mission that He had sent me to accomplish.

To finish my story, moments after my translator nervously asked if I had a word, an entourage of finely dressed men entered the room, complete with a camera crew. We stood and welcomed them, shaking hands with each one as they took their seats. It became evident right away that they were unsure about what exactly we were supposed to be doing.

A friend of mine who knew this national leader had previously asked him if he had any interest in meeting with a "futurist" (rather than using the word *prophet*). My friend explained to this leader that a futurist is a person who has a special gift from God. A futurist would know his future and would be able to help him develop a strategic plan to succeed in the leadership of his country.

The leader told my friend yes, he would be interested in meeting a futurist (me), but that he would only have thirty minutes to do so. I think thirty minutes must be the magic number, since most political leaders give us only half an hour to speak to them the first time we meet.

The next thing I knew, I was sitting in this ornate room in another country, and the media people who had come in had set up a map of the country as a backdrop for filming. The cameras started rolling as I made small talk with the national leader for a few minutes while I was waiting for God to give me a prophetic word. My translator was growing increasingly tense as time passed, but I had a deep sense of peace that seemed to cover me like a blanket.

Finally, I got a vague picture of this leader holding hands with two young girls who were both six years old, so I said to him, "I see you holding hands with two young girls who are six years old. But you don't have two daughters, do you?"

"No, I don't," he responded through the translator.

"That's right, because the vision means that six years ago you were instrumental in bringing women into this male-dominated political world because you believe in women.

In fact, you hate the oppression of women in your country. You're a champion for them!" I said confidently.

"That is exactly right!" he responded excitedly to the translator.

"You have a pure heart and have always wanted to do the right thing since you were a little boy," I proclaimed. "That's why God put you in this position, because He knows He can trust you," I continued.

Then I shared some specific things about his childhood with him that only he and God would know about. This leader was noticeably shaken, and I could feel his heart opening up to us.

"Can a good man suddenly become a bad man?" he asked intently.

"Yes," I responded. "But God forgave you for the bribe you took nine months ago," I added in a fatherly voice, "so you should forgive yourself, too."

We stared at each other as my translator slowly interpreted my answer to him. Then suddenly, everyone stood up abruptly as the leader forcefully demanded that they all leave the room. I looked down at the timer I had set for thirty minutes and realized that we only had about seven minutes left of our meeting. Now he was obviously nervous, and I could detect fear in his eyes.

This leader's voice quivered as he asked, "What else do you know?"

"I know that there is another bribe on your desk, and that if you take that bribe, you will be removed from your office because you will be caught," I said, staring intently into his eyes.

Again my translator seemed hesitant to interpret my message to him. But a moment later, the leader's eyes filled with tears as I reminded him that God believes in him.

"I won't take the bribe—I won't!" he said, with his hands shaking.

I looked down at my timer that indicated just two minutes were left. I stood up and thanked him for the meeting.

"I know you are a very busy man. Thank you so much for giving us your time," I said with a smile.

When I got ready to leave, the leader asked me if I could stay for a while longer. I assured him that I could, and we spoke for another two hours. He kept calling his secretary and telling her to cancel the next meeting.

Several times during our conversation, I said, "You probably need to get back to work," and I began to stand up.

"No, no, I am really enjoying this conversation," he replied through my translator. "Please stay and tell me more of what God showed you about my life."

Over time, I built a professional relationship with this leader. Whenever I am in his country now, he flies to any city I am in to meet with me. He is just one of many world leaders whom I have built a relationship with, or at least have ministered to prophetically over the years.

Time Is on Their Side

One of the things I have learned about ministering to leaders is that they are all overly busy and everyone wants their time. Whether they are involved in government, the corporate world or the Church, time is their most valuable commodity. It is imperative that when you or I meet with them, we do not take one minute more than they have agreed to in a meeting. It is also important that they know we value their time by the fact that we are keeping track of how long our meeting is going.

No matter how well you think your interaction with a high-level leader is going, you should always stand up and initiate the close of the meeting so that they do not have to. Sometimes we can think a meeting is going well, when in fact the leader is just being polite. Political leaders are especially used to being diplomatic and gracious, so it is easy to mistake their kindness for receptivity.

If leaders have more time available for you than they allotted, or if something so powerful is happening in their lives through your prophetic ministry that they want to cancel their next meeting, that is their decision. But many times they are unable (or unwilling) to prolong a meeting, so it is up to you to steward the time you do have with them. This means that right from the start, you must allocate your meeting time wisely and not waste it on meaningless conversation. Be kind and caring, but get to the point as soon as possible. If leaders grant you more time or ask you to stay, find out how much more time they are willing to spend with you and again steward the time by paying attention to your watch.

Always be early for your appointment with a leader. *Never, never* make leaders wait for you. Personally, I have lost count of the number of times that people wait three months to get an appointment with me and then show up late. Or they make small talk for 25 minutes and then finally get to the point with only five minutes of our scheduled time left. And nothing is more frustrating as a leader than to stand up and let people know their appointment is over, only to have them continue sitting right where they are and talking. Or they will get up and head to the door as if they are leaving, but then rudely stand in your doorway and keep you engaged in conversation for several more minutes beyond their appointment time.

To be honest, if I can help it I never have a second meeting with someone who does not value my time. I have never known a great leader who does not have more to do in a day than he or she can get done. Remember that you may be a laid-back person or someone who has plenty of time on your hands, but most leaders do not have the luxury of either wasting time or having you waste their time.

Lessons from the Palace

If you and I are going to minister to busy and influential leaders, we need to set some important ground rules for ourselves so that our ministry is both welcome and effective. Here are nine more lessons I have learned about ministering to high-level leaders:

1. Manage your appetites. King Solomon said it best: "When you sit down to dine with a ruler, consider carefully what is before you, and put a knife to your throat if you are a man of great appetite. Do not desire his delicacies, for it is deceptive food" (Proverbs 23:1–3). It is important that each of us know what we have an appetite for so we can manage it proactively. For example, if you have an appetite for fame but you refuse to acknowledge it, then you will not proactively manage your appetite. Instead, it will manage you. Most often, the fact that you and I have an appetite for something is not in itself evil. Temptation is not sin. Jesus Himself was tempted in every way, except He was without sin (see Hebrews 4:15). What you and I do with our appetites is paramount. Solomon's exhortation reminds us to manage our desires proactively, especially when we are in the presence of powerful people.

2. Confidentiality is of the utmost importance, especially with world leaders. Never share in a public setting what went on in your personal conversation with a leader,

not even as a testimony or privately with people who cannot be trusted with secrets. Even the fact that you met with someone important should be kept private. This means that if you are using a translator, he or she must also be sworn to secrecy and be trustworthy. Do not ever put these meetings on your itinerary where the public can see them. Never make any comments to the media about what did or did not happen in a meeting with a leader. The career of political leaders depends on confidentiality. What may seem like incidental information to you could destroy their credibility and ruin their career.

3. Do not ask to take pictures with famous people. Social networking has created an atmosphere where prominent leaders are gun-shy about having their photographs taken with people. Often, flaky people will try to show their friends that they are important by posting a picture of themselves with a famous leader on some social media site. Unfortunately, the world often views this as the leader being guilty by association. You might be a person of great integrity, but your differing political, moral or religious beliefs may cost that leader his or her credibility. I am not famous, but people ask to take pictures with me all the time. I do not mind having my picture taken with people, but sometimes my photograph ends up on some website or on the social network page of someone who does not represent my views or moral standards at all. To make matters worse, once something is on the Internet, it is there virtually forever.

4. Do not ask leaders for their contact information. Give them yours so that if they want to get in touch with you, they know how. Most leaders are very protective of their private information such as their personal cell number and/or their private email address. Asking them for this information puts them in an awkward situation. Likewise, if they offer you their private information,

and you later send them a message to which they do not respond, take the hint. They are either too busy to respond, or they are not interested in developing a relationship with you. Do not keep hounding them. Also, never give a leader's private information to anyone else. If someone wants to get in touch with a leader whom you know, contact the leader yourself and relay your friend's contact information.

5. Cell phones and the Internet are not secure communication devices. Many world leaders' phones are tapped, and their emails are hacked. I am not paranoid; I actually have been in situations with political leaders where we found out later that our conversation was bugged. Let me put it this way: It wasn't pretty!

6. Dress appropriately. It is typically better to be over-dressed than underdressed. Most of the time, I wear a suit and tie to meetings with political and business leaders. Ladies, although it is important that you wear a dress or business suit, it is more important that you dress modestly. Make sure that you understand the customs and traditions of the people you are meeting with so that you do not offend them with your clothing.

7. Many leaders whom you and I may meet with have no understanding of supernatural ministry, nor do they understand the "Christianese" language or various religious terms. If you are prophesying to someone or speaking to them about God, do it in a vocabulary they can understand. Using words like *anointing*, *repentance*, *mantle*, etc. usually puts a leader who is in government or the business world at a disadvantage. They are often afraid to reveal their ignorance and therefore will not ask you what it is you are trying to communicate. Unlike Christians in a charismatic church setting, most of these people have no way to judge whether your prophetic words are accurate or not, meaning they literally have

no safety net. That is why it is really important that you are sure of the prophetic direction you are giving to these leaders. If you are wrong, at best they probably will never meet with you again. But if they act on an inaccurate prophetic word, it could be devastating. Make sure that they understand what it is you are trying to say and how they can apply it to their lives. If the prophetic word is veiled in some kind of metaphorical vision or dream, clearly interpret it for them. If you do not understand the vision or dream yourself, it is probably best to not share it with them.

8. Scrap all your agendas. Do not meet with high-level leaders if your sole agenda is to lead them to Christ. They will feel as if you are a car salesman and they have just stepped onto a car lot. Just love them and let your life be a message to them. It is unwise to use your access to a leader to promote your social, political, spiritual or moral agenda. Also, do not use prophecy to correct a leader's stand on various issues. For example, if you are pro-life and the leader you are meeting with is pro-abortion, do not trust any prophetic word you have that would correct his or her opinion. You are too invested in your core perspective to maintain enough objectivity to prophetically direct someone on an issue that you feel passionate about. Honestly, it is spiritual manipulation when we use our prophetic gift to correct someone's moral values. We should not do with prophecy what we should be doing with discipleship. If a leader opens his or her heart to you and asks for your opinion on an issue, then feel free to share your heart. But otherwise, let your character, wisdom and love speak for themselves.

9. Learn the language of Babylon. Remember how Daniel was taught the literature and language of the Chaldeans? It is important that we understand the customs, history and core perspectives of the leaders to whom we

are ministering. Some countries are very sensitive to certain titles. For various reasons, the title "Christian" has a negative connotation in many countries. Muslims view Christians as the enemies who committed so many atrocities throughout the Crusades. Atheists often view Christians as anti-intellectual or superstitious. The title "Christian" has been so misused over the last two thousand years that to most people, it hardly represents the teachings of Jesus anymore. Personally, I tell every leader who asks me about my religious beliefs that I am a "follower of Jesus." We were always called to be followers of Jesus anyway. Jesus never called us Christians. My larger point, however, is that it is important that we are culturalized into the countries in which we are called to disciple.

A New World of Prophetic Realities

God is calling us as noble prophets and prophetesses, who are comfortable in the courts of kings (and who also love the poor and broken), to understand the epoch season in which we live, so that we can rise up and positively influence the course of history. He has empowered us to cast off the shackles of judgment and begin to prophesy constructively to the hurting, wounded and depressed. God has also commissioned us as His New Testament prophets and prophetesses to train and equip the King's royal army of saints so that they can displace darkness and build with light.

Some of us may never grace the threshold of a palace or dine with a world leader, yet we are still called to speak for the King so that we can bring hope to the hopeless and courage to the fainthearted. It is in the darkest situations that we must call for light, it is in the dirtiest souls that we must look for treasure and it is in the toughest of times that we must strengthen the weary.

William H. Mauldin (an American cartoonist) wrote, "I feel like a fugitive from the law of averages." He is right. We were not created to be average or mediocre. We have been summoned by God and empowered by His Spirit to step out of the crowd and be counted among the brave. We must refuse to hide among the riskless, mindless, zombielike flock. We must put on the mind of Christ and expose the world to the supernatural wisdom of the ages—wisdom that stuns the intelligent, silences the critics and transforms our cities and nations.

Jesus said that we are to make disciples of all nations and teach them the ways of the Kingdom. Abraham was promised that he would be the father of many nations and that his descendants would be as numerous as the stars in the sky and the sands of the sea. The great apostle John heard a voice from heaven saying, "The kingdom of the world has become the kingdom of our Lord and of His Christ; and He will reign forever and ever" (Revelation 11:15). This is our prophetic mission, our mandate and our passion. My prayer is that it be on earth as it is in heaven! I dare you to leave the shores of predictable living and join us as we set sail on the journey to a new world of prophetic realities.

Index

to world leaders, 223–25
See also prophetic ministry, primary
lessons of
prophetic ministry, primary lessons of,
225–30
avoid agendas, 228
importance of confidentiality in,
225–26
learn the language of "Babylon,"
228–29
managing of appetites, 225
proper use of cell phones and the
Internet, 227
refuse to ask leaders for contact
information, 226–27
refuse to take pictures with leaders,
226
use the proper vocabulary, 227–28
wear the appropriate dress, 227
prophetic revelation, 166–67
prophets/prophetesses, 44–45, 85, 110,
217
acknowledging the office of, 30–31
and the Body of Christ, 142–43
as builders, 137–38
and the commissioning of leaders,
144–47
different types/personalities of, 211–14
and empowerment and confrontation,
171–76
and the equipping of the saints,
138–43
as the eyes of the Body of Christ,
85–86
God's calling of, 210–11
God's protection of, 151–54
leadership role of, 32
prophetic perspectives, 79–81
and the protection of nations, 154–55
role of, 131–35
spirits of, 171
and the transformation of nations,
189–90
See also New testament prophets;
Old Testament prophets; prophetic
ministry; prophets/prophetesses,
office of

prophets/prophetesses, office of, 118–19
anointing of, 121–22
being called to, 120–21
differences between the gift of
prophecy and the office of prophecy,
122–23
and the gift of prophecy, 119–20
restoration of by God, 143–44
Protestants, Pentecostal, 16, 17
beliefs concerning the Holy Ghost,
17–18
prophesying of, 17

Rachel, 190
reconciliation, 66–67
revelation, new versus old, 115–17
"revelation bump," the, 78
righteousness, 54, 55
risk, 163–69
balancing of, 167–68
Romney, Mitt, 156
Russia/Russians, 159, 209

Samuel, 31, 144–45, 212
meeting with Saul, 188–89
Sapphira, 67–70
Sarah, 151–52
Saul, 32, 144
meeting with Samuel, 188–89
seeing, and "damaged lenses," 81–82
signs and wonders, 94
Silk, Danny, 77
sin/wickedness/evil, 41–42, 70
as falling short of the glory of God,
91
God's hatred of, 43
Greek definition of, 82
overcoming evil, 93
See also money, love of as evil
social networking, 35, 226
Solomon, 174, 225
on counseling people, 175–76
spatial disorientation, 84–85
*Spirit Wars: Winning the Invisible
Battle against Sin and the Enemy*
(Vallotton), 32, 96
spiritual warfare, 95–96

Kris Vallotton has been happily married to his wife, Kathy, since 1975. They have four children and eight grandchildren. Three of their children are in full-time vocational ministry. Kris is the co-founder and senior overseer of the Bethel School of Supernatural Ministry, which has grown to more than two thousand full-time students. He is also the founder and president of Moral Revolution, an organization dedicated to cultural transformation.

Kris is the senior associate leader of Bethel Church in Redding, California, and has served with Bill Johnson since 1978. He has written and co-authored numerous books, and his revelatory insight and humorous delivery make him a much-sought-after international conference speaker.

You can contact Kris or find out more about him and his other ministry materials at www.kvministries.com, or you can download the KV ministries app on your smartphone. You can also follow Kris and Kathy on their Facebook fan page at www.facebook.com/kvministries.

More from Bethel Leaders

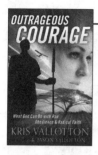

From treating rebel guerillas in Asia to sipping tea in a Mozambican hut while bullets whistled through the walls, Tracy Evans—a friend of the Vallotton family—has followed God's call into very dangerous places. In this book, you'll discover what God can do through one person's radical obedience.

Outrageous Courage by Kris Vallotton and Jason Vallotton

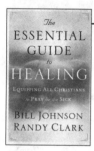

The ministry of healing is *not* reserved for a select few. In this practical, step-by-step guide, Bill Johnson and Randy Clark show how you, too, can become a powerful conduit of God's healing power.

The Essential Guide to Healing by Bill Johnson and Randy Clark

Don't settle for a defeated, powerless existence. In this book, bestselling author Eric Johnson reveals how to move beyond the limitations we place on ourselves and God, and live with passion, power and purpose.

Christ in You by Eric Johnson

✔Chosen